Advance Praise

A masterpiece in intercultural training!

Exploring Culture is a very valuable introductory book in the area of cross-cultural psychology and cross-cultural training. The use of ten synthetic cultures along with various exercises for improving cross-cultural awareness should be particularly valuable for managers and trainers interested in cross-cultural issues.

—Rabi S. Bhagat, Ph.D.
Professor of Org'l. Behavior and Int'l. Management,
Karen Moustafa, Ph.D. student in management,
University of Memphis

The authors of Exploring Culture…provide both professionals and curious readers with a clear menu for cultural analysis along with a varied buffet of stories, examples, exercises and simulations that both nourish understanding and fortify intercultural competence.

—George F. Simons, Ph.D.
George Simons International
www.diversophy.com

This book bridges theory and practice through a series of hands-on exercises that help the reader to develop greater understanding of Hofstede's conceptual framework. It is an engaging book that will be a valuable tool for any cross-cultural trainer, intercultural educator, or student of culture.

—Kenneth Cushner Ed.D.
Associate Dean and Professor
Kent State University

Exploring Culture

Gert Jan Hofstede, Paul B. Pedersen, Geert Hofstede

Exploring Culture

Exercises, Stories and Synthetic Cultures

INTERCULTURAL PRESS
A Nicholas Brealey Publishing Company

BOSTON • LONDON

First published by Intercultural Press, a Nicholas Brealey Publishing Company, in 2002. For information contact:

Intercultural Press, Inc., a division of Nicholas Brealey Publishing 20 Park Plaza, Suite 610 Boston, MA 02116 USA Tel: +(617)-523-3801 Fax: +(617)-523-3708

Nicholas Brealey Publishing 3-5 Spafield Street, Clerkenwell London, EC1R 4QB, UK Tel: +44-207-239-0360 Fax: +44-207-239-370

www.nicholasbrealey.com

Cover art Ten Puppets puzzle, interior puzzle piece, and line art by Gert Jan Hofstede

ISBN-13: 978-1-877864-90-2
ISBN-10: 1-877864-90-0
Printed in the United States of America
16 15 14 13   9 10 11 12

Hofstede, Gert Jan.
    Exploring culture: exercises, stories, and synthetic cultures/Gert Jan Hofstede, Paul B. Pedersen, Geert H. Hofstede.
        p. cm.
    Includes bibliographical references and index.
    1 Cross-cultural orientation. 2. Intercultural communication. 3. Culture shock. 4. Cultural awareness. I. Pedersen, Paul, 1936– II. Hofstede, Geert H. III. Title.

GN345.65.H63 2002
306–dc21   2002068505

Table of Contents

Foreword

Since the beginning of recorded time, people from different cultures have met to trade, marry, and make war. After two devastating world wars and with the dawning of the nuclear era, knowledgeable people around the world have begun to realize that warfare is becoming too destructive and that the cost is too high. Institutions such as the European Community and NAFTA as well as the Japanese constitution, are examples of attempts at international cooperation.

But international cooperation turned out to be beset with miscommunication. Thus, starting in the 1960s a new field of training, intercultural communication, was born. Its primary goal was to train people from different cultures to get along better with one another. Today awareness of the concepts of intercultural communication is more urgent than ever. This book constitutes a step forward in cross-cultural training. Allow me to explain this from my academic vantage point. Over time a variety of hypotheses were generated (e.g., Landis and Bhagat 1996). A few were tested with random assignment of participants, some of whom received training and some of whom did not (see Brislin and Bhawuk 1999). The dependent variables were degrees of effectiveness of the trainee when working with others, the perceptions of the trainee by members of the host cultures, the culture shock experienced by the trainee in the other culture, and similar variables.

In order to test the effectiveness of some of these methods, numerous training methods were developed (e.g., Fowler and Mumford 1995; 1999). Up to the early 1980s the training schemas were not based on an empirically derived conceptual scheme. Hofstede's *Culture's Consequences* (1980) provided some of the dimensions for analyzing culture. Readers who wish to see the most recent empirical evidence and validity data concerning the Hofstede dimensions of cultural variation can consult the second edition of Hofstede's book (2001). Since 1980 countless publications have analyzed and synthesized aspects of culture using these dimensions.

Based on Hofstede's dimensions, other theories were developed about the way cultures can be compared. Some of these theories have been successfully incorporated into training programs. In fact it has been shown (Bhawuk 1998) that theory-based cross-cultural training is more effective than training that consists of scattered samples of beliefs, attitudes, and experiences. Why? It is easier for the learner to absorb the material and generalize to new situations if the training is based on theory.

Bhawuk's 1998 study contrasted cultures on only the identity (individualism–collectivism) dimension. Brislin and Bhawuk called for the use of all five of the Hofstede dimensions in future training: hierarchy (power distance), truth (uncertainty avoidance), gender (masculinity–femininity), and virtue (long-term/short-term perspective).

Exploring Culture presents training that uses all of Hofstede's dimensions. Thus, it is the next logical step in the development of cross-cultural training. The authors use the ten "synthetic cultures" invented by Paul Pedersen and Gert Jan Hofstede. These cultures consist of the attitudes, beliefs, positive and negative concepts, norms, rules, self-definitions, values, and the like typically found at the extreme poles of each of the five Hofstede dimensions.

The training material in this book comprises exercises, stories, and simulations. Parts I and II of the book can be studied by individuals, or all of the materials can be used by trainers working with individuals or teams.

Hofstede, Pedersen, and Hofstede use the didactic triad of awareness of culture as the set of social rules of a society, followed by knowledge of cultural patterns and then by skills in cross-cultural interaction. The synthetic cultures serve as vehicles for the knowledge and skills steps.

As each synthetic culture is sketched out, the authors mention the "obsessions" of each of the ten cultures (e.g., people in the individualist culture (Indiv) are obsessed with *freedom*), the core distinctions, the golden rules, and the concepts that are positive and negative in each culture. They list what stereotypes outsiders are likely to have about each of the cultures, how people are likely to behave under stress in each, and so on.

There is a very sophisticated discussion about the way culture influences how people get along with one another. Many caveats are offered so the reader will not assume that "real" cultures are exactly like the synthetic cultures. Suggestions are offered on how to interview people from each of the synthetic cultures, along with many actual interviews using both sensitive and insensitive techniques.

The book also contains an excellent discussion of the advantages and disadvantages of simulations for learning about culture and provides details about how to select and prepare for simulations.

Finally, two simulations are presented in the book and more are made available on the Web. Extensive background is provided that reminds one of the case studies used in business schools.

In sum, this book provides superb material that can be used to become quite sophisticated in understanding, interacting with, and getting along with people from other cultures.

—Harry C. Triandis
Professor Emeritus
University of Illinois, Urbana-Champaign

Acknowledgments

Over one hundred thousand people have contributed to this book by filling in the original questionnaires that enabled Geert Hofstede to write *Culture's Consequences*. Since then, in the flow of knowledge, many others have influenced our thinking. These include all of our friends and students who contributed stories to this book, many of whom did the exercises and simulations and whose comments served to improve them. There is no end to the list of those we ought to thank.

But there are some people we wish to mention by name. In more or less chronological order, these are David Crookall, for asking Gert Jan to write the article in *Simulation and Gaming* that paved the way for the book; Erran Carmel, for cocreating the *Follow-the-Sun* simulation; Barbara Pirie, for rethinking the book structure with us; Harry Triandis, for agreeing to write the Foreword; Murray Thomas, for his wonderfully ambiguous pictures; and finally Judy Carl-Hendrick, for a first-class editorial process.

—Gert Jan Hofstede
Paul Pedersen
Geert Hofstede
July 2002

Introduction

If you are a cross-cultural trainer, educator, or student, *Exploring Culture* is for you. It is a playful book of practice, yet firmly rooted in Geert Hofstede's work on national culture. We introduce so-called *synthetic culture profiles* that bring Hofstede's dimensions of national culture to life in activities and simulations. The book intricately links culture theory and learning practice not only through the synthetic cultures but also through stories and exercises.

For students the many real-life exercises and stories, all with debriefings, make much of this book ideally suited for self-study. It is a very good companion to Geert Hofstede's textbook about national cultures, *Cultures and Organizations.**

For educators and trainers, this book also offers group exercises and simulations. It provides rich background reading, theoretical grounding in Geert Hofstede's five dimensions, and synthetic cultures. And if you are not looking for ready-to-use simulations but want to create your own, the book is a perfect starting point.

Gert Jan Hofstede is the primary author of *Exploring Culture*, but he "stood on the shoulders" of his co-authors. Geert Hofstede's extensive empirical research, from which he created his model for characterizing national cultures in five dimen-

---

* The first edition was published by McGraw-Hill in 1991. Various reprinted editions are available in English (1997) and in many other languages.

sions, is the intellectual basis for the book. The second source of inspiration is Paul Pedersen; he saw how Hofstede's dimensions could be used as a training tool for cross-cultural counselors and created four "synthetic cultures" (Pedersen and Ivey 1993). Working as an information systems researcher, Gert Jan saw how the era of globalization was changing his world and decided to use his father's work to create business gaming activities. He came across Paul's four synthetic cultures and added six more so that both extremes of each of the five culture dimensions were covered. The resulting model worked so successfully that Paul suggested creating a book for the community of cross-cultural students, trainers, and educators.

Exploring Culture balances understanding and doing, theory and practice. In chapter 1 we use stories and exercises to remind readers that our world is not really a "global village," even today. The book uses the triad of awareness–knowledge–skills to indicate the order of learning and hence the possible levels of goals for learners. In chapter 2 we explain why this is so by introducing the five basic problems of societies that constitute Geert Hofstede's dimensions of national culture: identity, hierarchy, gender, truth, and virtue. The chapter starts with a fairy tale that illustrates Geert Hofstede's five problems in a nutshell. Next come exercises that illustrate how the five dimensions of culture shape daily life. Finally, you will return to the exercises you did in chapter 1 and apply to them what you just learned about the dimensions of culture. Chapter 3 introduces the ten synthetic culture profiles: two for each of the five dimensions. Chapter 4 presents exercises to allow you to practice the synthetic cultures individually or in small groups. In chapter 5 you find twenty sample dialogues, two for each synthetic culture. One illustrates how an individual gives culturally insensitive feedback; another demonstrates how a "perfectly acculturated" member from each synthetic culture might behave during a dialogue. If you are interested in cross-cultural interviewing skills for business or counseling, you will find this chapter especially interesting. Finally, chapter 6 sums up the learning that you can gather from Parts I and II of the book.

Exploring Culture balances understanding and doing, theory and practice.

Culture resides in groups of people. That is why group exercises and simulation games are such a good way to learn about cross-cultural encounters. Part III of the book consists of material for trainers who work with groups of people. Chapter 7 provides a step-by-step procedure on how to use this book as a framework for cross-cultural learning for group participants and introduces three small-group exercises as well as the Synthetic Culture Laboratory, which is a customizable, general-purpose simulation. In chapter 8 we give an overview of the ways in which simulation games have addressed cross-cultural issues, we present the justification of synthetic culture profiles as a means to bring the five dimensions of culture to life in simulation games, and we give advice on how to create or select, prepare, run, and debrief simulations using the synthetic cultures. Chapters 9 and 10 consist of two complete simulations, one simulating cross-cultural negotiation and the other, a globally distributed design team.

What This Book Is About

What do you think of the following statements?
- The world is essentially a global village.
- The world would be a better place if everybody behaved like the people in my country.
- One could live in any country in the world, if one were honest and well-intentioned.
- Business is business in any country.
- Children's upbringing at home and their lives in school and later in the workplace are unrelated.
- National cultures will be a thing of the past fifty years from now and beyond.

If you agree with any of these statements, read on. Do the exercises. Participate in the simulations. Then return to these statements and reconsider your responses.

As you may have guessed, we, the authors of this book, agree with none of the statements. We believe that people from

National culture is the name we give to that which distinguishes the people of one country from those of another.

different countries are usually more different from one another than are people from the same country. *National culture* is the name we give to that which distinguishes the people of one country from those of another. National culture runs deep. It is taught to children from the day they are born. Does it matter whether a child is female or male? What about social class? Do children accompany their mothers all day? Does the family sleep in one room or even in one bed? Do grown-ups teach their children to use different behavior toward the elderly, the young, men, women? To stand up and fight or to sit down and talk? To speak their mind or to save others' face? To wear skirts, shorts, veils, caps? Or are all these things theirs to decide, and if so, from what age?

Whether we world citizens enjoy it or not, most of us interact with people from other countries ever more frequently. We meet tourists and we are tourists. We work in multinational organizations. We strike trade deals. We conduct diplomacy. We learn how people across the world are interconnected through the flow of goods, money, knowledge, religious ideologies, weapons, diseases, sports teams, and tourists.

Cross-cultural misunderstanding is a much-underestimated cause of trouble. If we inhabitants of the globe do not acquire an awareness of our mutual differences, knowledge of basic cultural variables, the skills to communicate effectively across boundaries and the will to do so, our world will be the worse for it. We need to communicate effectively with people who were raised in ways utterly unlike our own.

Learning about cross-cultural communication can also be an immensely enriching experience. It can cause you to consider daily rituals and unquestioned assumptions in a new light, and it can add fun, excitement, and friends to your life.

This book will help you meet the combined intellectual and emotional challenge that is involved in learning to communicate across cultures. The intellectual challenge is understanding the essence of national culture: the rules of the social game that differ across borders. The emotional challenge is being

The intellectual challenge is understanding the essence of national culture: the rules of the social game that differ across borders. The emotional challenge is being able to put yourself in the place of somebody from a "strange" country.

EXPLORING CULTURE

able to put yourself in the place of somebody from a "strange" country.

One caveat must be mentioned before we begin. Much of what happens among people from different countries depends on culture, but not everything. First, to some extent every human being is unique. No two people behave in exactly the same manner, because of their character and personal history. Second, people are social beings, and they learn how to be so through the groups in which they participate. The likelihood that they will act in a particular manner in a particular social setting varies with group characteristics. For most people, their country of birth is a very important indicator of their socialization. For immigrant or ethnic populations within countries, this may be their forefathers' country of birth or a mix of both.

Finally, to some extent all people are alike. We all have the capacity to communicate with other people, however unlike ourselves they might be, and to learn to understand them. We hope that this book will help you develop this capacity to the fullest and that it will stimulate and enrich you.

We all have the capacity to communicate with other people, however unlike ourselves they might be, and to learn to understand them.

Part I
Stories and Exercises

Chapter 1

Worlds Apart in One Village

Some say we are all living in a "global village." This expression was popular in the Western world before 11 September 2001. But if proof need still be given, this chapter will make it clear that our global village has many disparate quarters. It shows how intercultural encounters can generate misunderstandings or worse. The chapter consists of stories and exercises for either individual or group work.

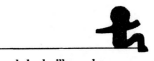

Our global village has many disparate quarters.

The following story illustrates that misunderstandings between people from different countries can both be sudden and have far-reaching consequences.

Since the end of World War II, Korea has been split in two parts. North Korea has become the devastatingly poor communist Democratic People's Republic of Korea. South Korea has become a comparatively rich capitalist state and has a U.S. military presence. Until the year 2000, these twin countries waged a fierce ideological battle against one another. The government of the United States sided with South Korea and had North Korea on its list of seven terrorist nations, the so-called "rogue states," because of incidents that had happened in the 1970s and 1980s. In 2000 the two Koreas started to talk about reconciliation or even reunification. This, then, is the background for the following incident.

The Frankfurt Incident

On the fourth of September 2000, in the last year of the Clinton administration, a North Korean delegation heads from Europe toward the United Nations millennium summit in New York. The delegation includes the country's vice leader, Kim Yong Nam. In New York the delegation is supposed to have a reconciliatory meeting with the president of South Korea.

Changing their prior travel plans, they choose an American airline at Frankfurt Airport. While the North Koreans are waiting for the plane, the airline's security personnel notice them. Following their instructions for members of rogue states who do not have diplomatic immunity, they call out these people and thoroughly search them. The North Koreans are very, very angry and fly home instead of going to the U.N. summit. The incident immediately hits the world press.

The North Korean ambassador, Mr. Li, recounts his version of the story: U.S. aviation security officials came up to the delegation and performed hooligan acts: questioning them and checking their luggage and stripping them to do a body search. They justified this conduct by saying that North Korea was listed as a rogue state and that they had instruc-tions from home to act as they did. Mr. Li concludes that the incident was purposely and insidiously created by the United States to hinder the reconciliation of the two Koreas, demonstrating that the U.S. is a rogue state itself.

A White House spokesman explains that because the delegation had changed its travel plans, the American airline personnel at Frankfurt Airport did not know who they were. They had done no more than follow the U.S. rules for rogue states, and the U.S. government had not been involved in the incident at all. The airline immediately apologizes and takes responsibility.

Various U.S. diplomats express regret about the incident. Four days later U.S. Secretary of State Madeleine Albright sends a formal letter of apology to the Northern Korean foreign minister and receives a reply that could be called conciliatory. In this reply North Korea says it has noted the American apology and shall watch the future deeds of the Americans but also states that its sovereignty has been injured and that "the Democratic People's Republic of Korea values its sovereignty like its life and soul."

The two Koreas resume their talks.

What happened at the airport was a very clear case of culture clash. Experienced travelers know that U.S. security personnel at airports tend to be heavy-handed regardless of whom they deal with. That fits with the American culture. They may not have been particularly polite to the North Korean delegation. In addition Americans hold the view that everybody is his or her own person, and one cannot hold the government responsible for the behavior of employees of some company as long as they stick to the rules. The North Koreans, on the other hand, come from a country where respect for authority is very important. Moreover, an insult to one North Korean is an insult to all. Looked at from this vantage point, the beleaguered security officials didn't just search a few strangers, they insulted a whole nation! This is evident in the emotional and nationalistic overtones of the North Korean reaction.

So you see that it is possible to explain the behavior of both sides in terms of their own way of thinking and come up with two widely different interpretations. Do you think either the American airline's officials or the North Korean delegation members learned anything from the incident? The Americans probably feel that the North Koreans are blowing this thing up ridiculously, while the North Koreans are now quite certain that Americans are savages. The media on both sides are likely not to have corrected this image.

Fortunately, in this case highly placed politicians on both sides were anxious to put the incident behind them. In many other cases an incident such as this one might have been the beginning of armed combat.

Awareness, Knowledge, Skills

If you were a high-level airline security official, what could you do to prevent similar incidents from happening in the future? Logically, it takes three steps to do this, to be taken in chronological order.

- Make your personnel *aware* that they differ from many foreigners in their social behavior and assumptions.

- Help them learn to *know* their differences from people from various parts of the world.
- Teach them the *skills* needed to communicate effectively with these various foreigners.

There is actually a fourth step, one that is needed throughout the process: motivate them to want to treat people from any country in a way that those people appreciate.

It can safely be assumed that the members of the North Korean delegation at Frankfurt have made it clear in their own way that they did not appreciate the safety measures. With sufficient training, the security people might have been aware of the possibility for misunderstanding, found out who these people were, and treated them with more cultural sensitivity.

The logical sequence of awareness, knowledge, and skills is the basis for this book. Activities and exercises are usually aimed at the awareness and knowledge steps. Simulation games are strong in the latter two areas; you practice intercultural communication skills, and you experience how it feels to be a foreigner. This experience can be very motivating. But we will start by working on awareness and knowledge.

What Do You See?

Consider the following set of pictures. Look at each picture briefly and write down what you think it might show. Then— and only then—read on and find out how a number of other people interpreted the picture. These people ranged in age from fourteen to fifty and came from Bolivia, China, Ethiopia, France, Indonesia, Italy, the Netherlands, Peru, Tunisia, and Uganda. Perhaps your own interpretation is on the list, perhaps not. As you will see, the pictures have an amazing number of possible interpretations, which differ because people concentrate on different aspects. Some look for unique attributes of the people in the picture. Others look for family relationships or for hierarchical relationships. Still others look for gender differences, for cooperation, for antagonism, or for details that highlight professional or religious roles. Try to figure out what attributes influenced your interpretation.

The lesson to be drawn from this activity is that just by looking at a situation, you cannot tell what is happening. Unconsciously, you bring your own cultural frame of interpretation to any situation. This is not to say that culture alone determines how one interprets a picture or a situation. One's own unique history and personality also play an important role. But some of the interpretations made by people from other parts of the world probably seem very strange to you.

Unconsciously, you bring your own cultural frame of interpretation to any situation.

Picture 1

Possible interpretations:

- Two women are walking and a man threatens one of the women with a piece of wood
- Two men are attacking a woman
- A woman steps aside to let a blind man pass
- A beggar and a woman
- Gardening
- A farm family working on their land
- Two people helping each other do something
- Poor people. The man is digging for something and the woman is waiting to take it
- A man cleaning the floor
- A man is digging a hole and a woman is dropping seeds in it

Picture 2

Possible interpretations:

- A teacher reprimanding a student
- A man teaching other men
- A boss giving instructions to employees
- A government official warning a gathering of people with different religions
- Blessing
- A preacher in church
- A film director instructing his crew where to stand for the next scene
- A salesman trying to sell his wares

Picture 3

Possible interpretations:

- Prayer before a meal; two people do not want to pray
- People thinking hard to solve some problem
- Difficult conversation
- A meeting about to begin
- A family that has just received a sad letter
- A meeting. Two women on the left are talking on the side about a mobile phone
- The person on the left just bought some bread and is offering a piece to everybody
- People looking for a solution to some problem. The guy on the left is hiding the important evidence and showing something unimportant to the others
- The man in the middle presides over the debate. One guy is not involved
- A religious ritual

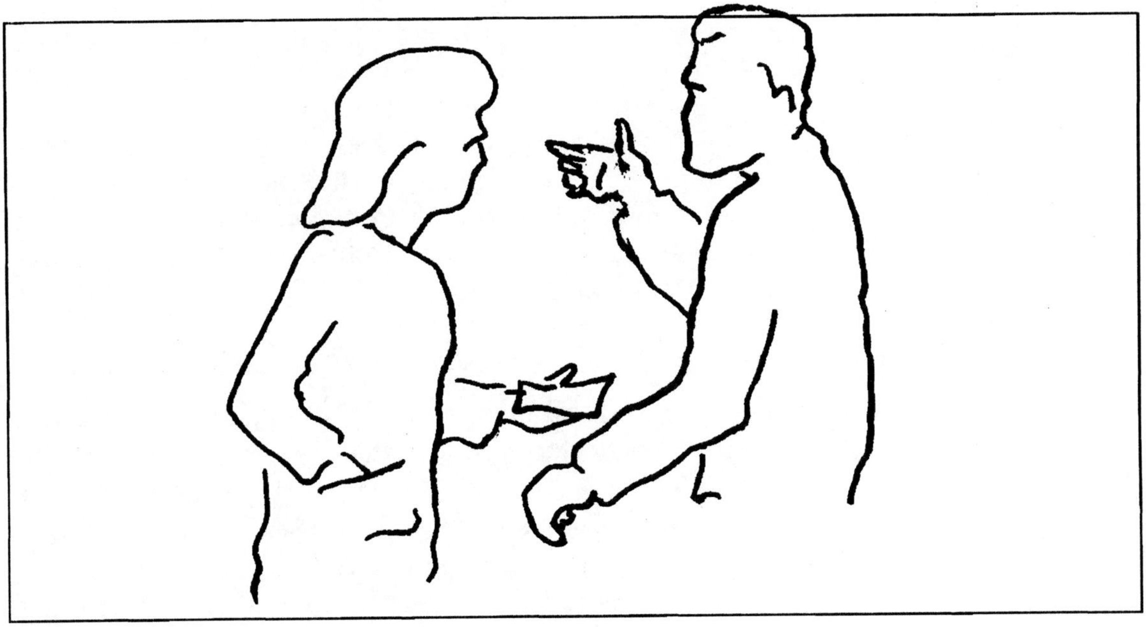

Picture 4

Possible interpretations:

- A woman is giving some money to a man and he is claiming he wants more money
- A woman trying to bribe a man
- A man is taking money from a woman
- A man is giving money to a woman. Something is problematic and they are discussing it
- Negotiation
- Educated people discussing something
- A woman asking the way and a man orienting her
- A discussion among friends
- A violent discussion
- A quarrel. She has insulted him in some way
- A lady giving her address to a man

Are you tempted to ask "But what do these pictures *really* mean?" We must confess that we deliberately asked the artist, Murray Thomas, to make ambiguous pictures that leave room for interpretation. So your interpretation is just as valid as anybody else's. Of course in a real social situation this is not so, because then you are facing real people with real intentions toward one another. We shall address some "real" situations in the following exercises.

How Would You Feel?

Here are some awareness exercises. They are short incidents in which you picture yourself interacting with somebody. That person's behavior stimulates expectations within you about his or her intentions toward you, or causes you to make moral inferences about the person. From a list of available responses to each incident, please choose one or more. Then try to figure out what values guided your choice. We will come back to the stories in chapter 2, when you will be in a position to interpret your responses from a cultural point of view.

The Shabby Guitar Player

You are in a restaurant having dinner with an acquaintance. A shabby man with a guitar comes to your table and offers to play. How do you feel about this?

1. This man is a beggar and should find a job.

2. This man is filthy and disgusting.

3. This man is to be pitied.

4. You do not know this man, and you have nothing to do with him.

5. Could be interesting. Maybe he plays well.

6. The waiter should remove this man.

A Meeting in the Street

You are walking along the street in a town that is not your own. The street is quiet. Somebody crosses the street and walks toward you. What do you think?

1. This person means to rob you.

2. This person means to ask for directions.

3. This person means to have a chat with you.

4. This person might invite you to dinner.

5. This person is going to tell you that you are not allowed to be here.

6. This person means to sell you something.

A Welcome at the Airport

You are headed to a formal business meeting with somebody you have never met before. When you get off the airplane, a warmly smiling woman wearing jeans and sandals is holding up a sign with your name on it. What do you think?

1. She must be a secretary.

2. She is probably the person with whom you will have the meeting.

3. It is wonderful to be welcomed so warmly.

4. How dare someone meet you in such an informal outfit.

5. There must be an error, because you were expecting a formal-looking gentleman.

The Intruder

You are standing at a reception, engaged in conversation with another person you vaguely know. Suddenly a third person arrives and starts to talk to your conversation partner without seeming to notice you. What do you think?

1. This must be a close friend of your conversation partner.
2. This must be an absolute brute to push you aside in this manner.
3. Your conversation partner should ask the intruder to wait a moment.
4. This must be a VIP (Very Important Person).
5. This must be somebody with a very urgent matter.
6. Your conversation partner should introduce you to the newcomer.
7. Nothing.

What Would You Do?

Here are four more short incidents. Read them and choose from the options how you would act. Then think about what values guided your choices. In some cases, different values might make you hesitate between different options. We will also come back to these stories in chapter 2, when you will be in a position to interpret your proposed action from a cultural point of view.

The Returning Athlete

You are the mayor of a small town. An athlete from your town took part in the Olympic Games. The athlete is due to return tomorrow, having obtained fourth place in an event. What sort of official welcome will you prepare for her?

1. None, because a fourth place is not worth anything. If only it had been a gold medal....

2. None, because there is no protocol for officially receiving returning sports players or participants.

3. A grand one, because even if she did not win, she did participate in the Olympic Games and that is a great achievement.

4. A grand one, because she is one of us and she has honored our town.

5. You will ask the city council for advice.

The Accident

You are chairing a very important business meeting, for which some attendees have made a transoceanic flight. Millions of dollars are involved. During the meeting one of your local colleagues, a financial expert, receives a message: his eight-year-old child has been hit by a car and is hospitalized with very severe injuries. How do you react?

1. You cancel the meeting and arrange for a sequel on the following day.

2. You let your colleague leave the meeting.

3. You leave the room for a moment with your colleague and tell him that although you would like him to stay, he can leave if he wants to.

4. You go on with the meeting, asking your colleague to stay.

Train or Car?

You are a commuter. The car trip to work takes approximately one hour, the train ride, approximately an hour and a half. Do you prefer to go by car or by train?

1. By car, because if I travel by train, people will think I can't afford a car.

2. By car, because it is faster.

3. By car, because it is private.

4. By car, because people in my position do not travel by public transport.

5. By train, because it is safer.

6. By train, because it allows me to get some work done while traveling.

7. By train, because I might meet interesting people.

8. By train, because it is better for the environment.

9. Either way is fine, whichever is cheaper in the long run.

A Virtual Contact

On the Web you have found the site of somebody you might want to start a business relationship with. How would you establish the first contact?

1. Write a formal, polite paper letter on your company's letterhead.

2. Send an e-mail starting "Dear Mr. so-and-so" and ending "Kind regards, X."

3. Send an e-mail starting "My name is X and I have a proposal that might interest you" and ending with your first name.

4. Have your secretary arrange a phone call.

5. Call the person on the phone yourself.

Observation and Interpretation

The core of intercultural awareness is learning to separate observation from interpretation. For instance, consider the following dialogue. Suppose that you are in a foreign country, looking for the train station, and meet a woman on the street.

You:	Excuse me.
She:	(pauses, looks at you fleetingly and walks on)
You:	(walk up next to her) Excuse me (she looks down). Do you know the way to the railway station?
She:	(points vaguely) Excuse me. Walk that way and turn left.
You:	(smiling) Thank you.
She:	(walks off in the other direction)

What would you make of this?

- She was afraid of you.
- She disliked you.
- She was being respectful to you.

Your response will depend on your prior experiences and your own country of origin. The usual reaction would be to forget her actual behavior but remember the *intention* that you attributed to her, for example, "She was afraid of me."

If you are cross-culturally aware, you remember her behavior and suspend your attribution of meaning until you know enough of her culture. Her looking away might indicate any of the three suggested intentions and maybe others. It might, for example, be gender-related, or looking people in the eye might be considered impolite in her country.

Cross-Cultural Communication Barriers

LaRay Barna (1982) has elaborated on the distinction between observation and interpretation in cross-cultural communication. Five areas of practice constitute potential barriers. In or-

The core of intercultural awareness is learning to separate observation from interpretation.

Postpone interpretation until you know enough about the other culture.

Language is much more than learning new vocabulary and grammar. It includes cultural competence.

Our culture has taught us to communicate through unspoken messages that are so automatic that we rarely even think about them.

Stereotypes are a major barrier to communicating across cultures.

der to overcome these barriers, postpone interpretation until you know enough about the other culture. In other words observe behavior but try not to attach attribution to it.

First, there is the obvious barrier of language differences. Language is much more than learning new vocabulary and grammar. It includes cultural competence: knowing what to say and how, when, where, and why to say it. Knowing a little of the foreign language may only allow you to make a "fluent fool" of yourself. Also, within the same language the same word may have a different meaning in different settings. Ways to decrease the language barrier are (1) learn the language, (2) find someone who can speak the language as an interpreter, and (3) ask for clarification if you are not sure what someone says.

Second, there is the area of nonverbal communication such as gestures, posture, and other ways we show what we feel and think without speaking. Our culture has taught us to communicate through unspoken messages that are so automatic that we rarely even think about them. An interviewer might put his or her own cultural interpretation on your hand gesture, facial expression, posture, clothing, physical closeness or distance, eye contact, or personal appearance, and that attribution may not be what you intended at all. Ways to cross the nonverbal communication barrier are (1) do not assume you understand any nonverbal signals or behavior unless you are familiar with the culture, (2) don't take a stranger's nonverbal behavior personally, even if it is insulting in your culture, and (3) develop an awareness of your own nonverbal communication patterns that might be insulting in certain cultures.

Third, stereotypes are a major barrier to communicating across cultures. We try to fit people into patterns based on our previous experience. We see pretty much what we want or expect to see and reject the possible interpretations that don't fit with what we expect. If we expect people from country X to be unfriendly to foreigners, we will probably interpret their behavior in that way. Steps to overcome this barrier resemble the

EXPLORING CULTURE

familiar triad, awareness-knowledge-skills, that we discussed earlier in the chapter: (1) make every effort to increase awareness of your own preconceptions and stereotypes of cultures you encounter, (2) learn about the other culture, and (3) reinterpret their behavior from their cultural perspective, adapting your own stereotypes to fit your new experiences.

A fourth barrier is the tendency to evaluate behavior from the other culture as good or bad, to make a judgment based on our own cultural bias. Evaluation has been called the third stage of how we attribute meaning. The first two, observation and interpretation, lead naturally to it. Different attitudes about, for instance, food and drink can cause misunderstanding as we evaluate them. Ways to decrease the tendency to evaluate are (1) maintain appropriate distance, (2) recognize that you cannot change a culture (or yourself) overnight, (3) do not judge someone from another culture by your own cultural values until you have first come to know them and their cultural values.

Do not judge someone from another culture by your own cultural values until you have first come to know them and their cultural values.

The fifth barrier is the high level of stress that typically accompanies intercultural interactions. Like every other unfamiliar experience, intercultural contact is likely to involve some stress. Ways you can decrease stress are to (1) accept the ambiguity of cross-cultural situations in which you are not sure what others expect of you or what you can expect of them, (2) work to reduce other intercultural barriers, and (3) be forgiving of others and yourself, giving both them and yourself the benefit of the doubt.

Like every other unfamiliar experience, intercultural contact is likely to involve some stress.

In intercultural encounters, then, there are several filters that can prevent us from accurately understanding what others are trying to communicate, and that can prevent others from accurately understanding what we are trying to communicate: our tendency to interpret and evaluate behavior before we understand it, and our willingness to stereotype groups of people, which prevents us from interpreting behavior accurately. When we are looking and listening, the remedy is to try and increase the range of our perception, to observe and suspend our interpretation (what we think) and evaluation (what we feel), and to ask for clarification when in doubt. When speaking, we should take care to clarify the intention behind our words and check to see if our message has come across correctly. In all cases, we should be prepared for surprises.

What happens if these precautions do not succeed is the subject of the next section.

Culture Shock

If two or more people from different countries meet and a misunderstanding arises, we call it a cultural misunderstanding. If such a misunderstanding escalates, like The Frankfurt Incident, it is called culture clash. This type of encounter frequently arises in international trade or diplomacy. If people are immersed in a foreign culture for a prolonged period, it can lead to a state of frustration called culture shock.

The following account is by a young man from the Netherlands who went to Belgium to study for some months.

If people are immersed in a foreign culture for a prolonged period, it can lead to a state of frustration called culture shock.

Kissing Gets Out of Hand

When I first came to the Université de Liège in September, I saw two girls kissing. I wondered whether that was usual. A few minutes later some more people came into the building. At that moment the kissing seemed to get seriously out of hand. I saw something I had never seen in my life: all the boys kissing girls, girls kissing boys, girls kissing girls, and even boys kissing boys! My God, what was happening here? Just thirty kilometers from my home university, I saw something that I had not expected at all—two boys kissing. I was sure they were homosexual. I knew kissing among boys was quite usual in Italy, but in Belgium? Seeing girls kissing all boys did not impress me positively either. Then when some of them came toward me I was afraid they would start to kiss me too. I almost ran away. They must have seen how scared I felt, because they just shook hands.

When I saw people kissing at later times, I did not feel so strange about it anymore. This was just different, not wrong. Kissing seemed to be considered as just another way for people to greet each other no matter what sex they belong to. But I will never get used to it.

Interpretation

This kissing story describes a mild incident that has some typical attributes of culture shock. The young man sees foreigners, among whom he will have to live for some time, kissing inappropriately and excessively. He tries to interpret this kissing in his own frame of reference and gets the uneasy feeling (evaluation) that these people are "abnormal," the boys acting like gays and the girls like nymphomaniacs. So he becomes uncomfortable. He is in fact not sure he will be able to cope if he has to interact with "these people."

He has observed behavior (kissing) that is different from that at home. He immediately interpreted that behavior as odd and evaluated it as abnormal, even scary. After having been immersed for some time in the new culture, he gets used to the kissing behavior of the host culture and realizes that it is only a different way of accomplishing a familiar ritual—greeting a friend, in this case.

What Is Culture Shock?

Culture shock is a profoundly personal experience and is not the same for two persons or for the same person during two different occasions. Yet people who have experienced culture shock will recognize most of the elements that we will discuss.

Culture shock is the process of initial adjustment to an unfamiliar culture. It is a more-or-less sudden immersion into a nonspecific state of uncertainty where the individual is not sure what is expected of him or her, nor of what to expect from other people. It can occur in any situation where an individual is forced to adjust to an unfamiliar social system where previous learning no longer applies. This need not necessarily be a new country. It could be a new school, town, organization, or family.

There are at least six indicators that one is experiencing culture shock:

1. Familiar cues about how others are supposed to behave are missing, or the familiar cues now have a different meaning.

2. Values that the person considers good, desirable, beautiful, and worthy are not respected by the host.

3. One feels disoriented, anxious, depressed, or hostile.

4. One is dissatisfied with the new ways.

5. Social skills that used to work do not seem to work any longer.

6. There is a sense that this horrible, nagging culture shock will never go away.

Culture shock is the process of initial adjustment to an unfamiliar culture.

Stages in Culture Shock

Culture shock is frequently described as a series of stages that a person goes through. This stage model does not describe each instance of culture shock accurately, and many versions of the model have been proposed, but it can serve as a reference model. These are the stages:

1. Honeymoon
   This is where the newly arrived individual experiences the curiosity and excitement of a tourist, but where the person's basic identity is rooted back home.

2. Disorientation
   This stage involves disintegration of almost everything familiar. The individual is overwhelmed by the requirements of the new culture and bombarded by stimuli in the new environment. One feels disoriented and experiences self-blame and a sense of personal inadequacy.

3. Irritability and hostility
   One typically experiences anger and resentment toward the new culture for its having caused difficulties and having been less adequate than the old familiar ways.

4. Adjustment and integration
   This involves integration of new cues and an increased ability to function in the new culture. One increasingly sees the bad and the good elements in both cultures.

5. Biculturality
   In this stage a person has become fluently comfortable in both the old and the new culture. There is some controversy about whether anyone can really attain this stage.

Exercises

Rui is a student from a Southern European country who has been studying for his Ph.D. in Northern Europe for six months. This is his story.

The Day after the Party

I can still remember sitting in the airplane about to start my new life. I was very excited about coming to this country and making new friends. But once I got to the university the first weeks were mostly filled with practical problems. I had to find a room, I had to buy books, I had to register for various things, and so on. I had expected to get more help with these things. My supervisor was always away on a foreign trip or at meetings. Then over the next weeks I started to get the feeling that the people here were cold. During the day they never seemed to have time for anything other than working. Contacts with the people from my apartment building were distant and superficial, and I didn't know how to change that. The best part of the week was calling home on Saturday nights.

Then one of the Ph.D. students got married and invited me to the wedding party. That was great. I got to know the people from the office and many others, and we had a lot of fun. They taught me their way of dancing, and I taught them my way. I finally went home thinking, "Now I know how to make friends in this country." But the next Monday morning they acted as if nothing had happened! They just said the usual "hi" in the corridor and went on with their work! I felt cold and lonely. What had I done wrong? Were they showing me I was just an outsider after all?

My misery must have shown on my face, because a few days later one of the Ph.D. students I had been dancing with came to me and asked me whether something was the matter. We talked about it, and she explained to me that this was normal behavior and that people made a clear distinction between work time and private time. This conversation made me feel a bit better. Since then, we have talked about these things every now and then, and she and a few others have become good friends. I am doing well now. Work organization is efficient here, and I am making good progress. I have noticed that people do take the time to talk about the content matter of my work when I ask them. I still feel, though, that the people here do not make the best of their lives, and I miss the warmth of home.

Question

Rui went through at least the first four of the five phases of culture shock: honeymoon, disorientation, irritability and hostility, and adjustment and integration. Can you recognize these phases in the text?

Debriefing

When Rui first arrived, he was clearly in the honeymoon stage. He had a sense of adventure but did not anticipate possible problems. He certainly did not think of the possibility that the people here might be different from the people at home.

Soon Rui started to feel that something was wrong. He received neither the guidance that he expected nor the amount of personal contact with his supervisor that he needed. Gradually, he started to feel disoriented and inadequate: "People were cold," "I didn't know how to change that." These feelings became even worse after the wedding party when his hopeful expectations that he was making new friends were not met. This is the stage of irritability and hostility.

The Ph.D. student who noticed his distress and talked to him about it helped him escape from his isolation. Some readers may have experienced casually inquiring after the well-being of an immigrant and suddenly being faced with a vehement outburst of emotion. This is a sign that the person in question is in a stage of disarray and needs help. In Rui's case, he now had somebody to relate to who could help him integrate his experiences. He was able to vent his frustration about his new country to her without being afraid that she would get angry. He was now in the adjustment and integration stage.

When Rui talks about his present situation, he begins to see some advantages to his new country and to understand what is appropriate behavior: "Work organization is efficient," "…when I ask them." He still misses home, though. He has now reached the integration stage.

An Able Secretary

Maria, a young woman from Latin America, and her husband have recently moved to the United States. Having little formal schooling, Maria has taken a job as an assistant secretary. After a few months her boss notices that she is conscientious and intelligent. He takes Maria aside and talks to her about the possibility of taking some training in accounting, which will give her access to higher-level, more responsible jobs in the organization.

She agrees to his proposals, and he leaves her with a brochure about courses that she could take. However, she does not take any action, despite occasional inquiry by the boss. Three months later the boss gets fed up with waiting and takes Maria to task about why she has still not decided about a course. After much fidgeting and looking down, she tells him that she likes her present job. The boss cannot see why someone would not jump at such a good opportunity, and his good opinion of Maria is largely lost. He feels he has done all he can and takes no further notice of Maria.

Questions

This story was told from the point of view of the boss. What stages of culture shock do you think Maria experiences during this episode? And what about her boss? Does he recognize these stages, and does he experience culture shock himself?

Debriefing

To her boss, Maria's words seemed to contradict her actions. She agreed to take courses but did not do anything about it. This might have made the boss suspect that there was something he didn't know about the situation, and he might have used some tact. When he asked her why she had not done anything about choosing a course, she became so obviously nervous that he noticed. That was a sure sign that something was bothering her. Yet he missed the occasion of inquiring into this and the opportunity to make an able secretary even more valuable to his organization. Perhaps worse, he did not have any idea that he had done something wrong, and if he had

had any prejudices about immigrants, this experience certainly did nothing to dispel them.

Had the boss made an effort, he might have seen that Maria did not in fact want a higher-level job because such a move would be very unusual in the country where she came from and it made her nervous. He might also have seen that Maria could not say no to his face, but that not taking action was a way for her to say no without having to insult him. He might have found a way to make Maria more valuable without scaring her, or at least to make her feel competent in her present job.

In this story Maria missed the bridge to the new culture that Rui found in his fellow Ph.D. student. The story leaves Maria in the disorientation stage of culture shock. She doesn't have a clue about what she did wrong. She is very frustrated that the boss is angry at her although she works so hard and diligently, and she is unable to communicate effectively to him about it. She may well develop hostile feelings toward her boss and her new country.

In this story we see how the lack of intercultural awareness can not only negatively affect an immigrant but also those who work with immigrants, or more generally, those who act as managers in intercultural settings.

Conclusion

In this chapter we have met various degrees of cross-cultural miscommunication, ranging from benign misunderstandings to serious clashes and profound culture shock.

The young Dutchman in the kissing story concluded "But I will never get used to it." Obviously, he did not get completely through the adjustment and integration stage of culture shock. In fact, few people do. Yet we have to integrate cultures if we are to function in a multicultural world. It simply will not do to presume that all foreigners will one day become like us.

In order to understand cross-cultural encounters better, we shall now investigate in what ways cultures can differ.

It simply will not do to presume that all foreigners will one day become like us.

Chapter 2

Culture: The Rules of the Social Game

So far, you have read about how the same situation can be perceived differently by people from different countries. In this chapter we shall examine the differences between countries in a systematic way. The chapter starts with a fairy tale about five cousins who grew up in different countries. Then it draws lessons from the tale. You will be able to immediately apply these lessons in a number of intercultural exercises taken from real life. Finally you will use what you've learned to revisit the exercises of chapter 1 and to analyze your own answers.

The Best Country, a Fairy Tale

On the island of Malaila there is an inn. It has been there for many generations. When this story started, it was run by a couple who took good care of it and made their guests feel at home. Foreign guests would come back year after year and send their friends.

The couple had five daughters who went to school and enjoyed meeting the guests of the inn, who told them about foreign lands. On weekends the family would hold a party for the guests, where the five girls would sing and dance.

When the oldest girl, Satu, had finished school she started to help at the inn. A young foreigner, who had stayed with them several times with his family, fell in love with her and she with him. When he came back to the inn the next year, they married, and she followed her husband back to his country.

By that time the second daughter, Dua, had just completed school, and she took her sister's place at the inn. Some time later she also fell in love with a young man who was their guest. She married him and went with him to his country.

The third girl, Tiga, took Dua's place, but like her older sisters, she also fell in love with a foreign guest, and after a time she too went abroad with her new husband.

And so it went with the fourth and fifth daughters, Ampat and Lima. The innkeeper and his wife were now alone, their family spread all around the globe. The daughters sent their friends to the inn, which their parents continued to run.

Many years later, when the daughters themselves had adult children in their different countries, the old innkeeper died. The daughters all flew back with their families for his funeral and wept over their beloved father. And after the funeral they sat together with their mother. It was decided that their mother would sell the inn to a young couple who had presented themselves and would come and live with one of her daughters. But with whom? Each daughter and son-in-law offered their house for Grandma to retire to. And Grandma asked her five eldest grandchildren to describe to her what life in each of the foreign countries would be like.

Satu's daughter said: "Grandma, you will love our country. We believe in the rights of the individual. We believe all people are different, and they have a right to be different. I can pursue my own interests, do my own thing, and nobody will stop me. I can have my own opinions, and nobody can prevent me from expressing them. I can choose my own friends, and I can vote for the leaders I like, and nobody can tell me otherwise."

"But how can you be anybody in your country?" asked Aunt Lima. "Doesn't who you are depend on where you came from and on the groups you belong to? How can you expect your people to be loyal to you if you are not loyal to them? And who will take care of Grandma when she needs help? Who takes care of your father's aged relatives?"

"And don't you get into many conflicts? said Aunt Ampat. "Do you really say everything

EXPLORING CULTURE

that is on your mind? Did you forget that maintaining harmony with your relatives and friends is the foundation of a civilized society? How can you work together or even do business with other people if you have not first established harmony with them?"

"In our country, we believe that honest people speak their mind," said Satu's daughter. "We don't waste time in social chitchat for harmony's sake. And we believe that you are what you make yourself to be. You are not what your family is or what your friends are. That also means that we do not automatically expect our family to take care of us. My father's relatives will not expect us to look after them. We will be happy to look after Grandma, and of course we take care of our children as long as they are small, but by the time they are grown, they will have learned to look after themselves. And we do not expect them to look after us when we are old."

"But do children in your country at least learn to play and share with each other?" Aunt Tiga looked shocked.

"Our children learn to be themselves," said Satu's daughter. "If they want to play with their brothers and sisters, they are free to do so, and if they want to make other friends, they are also free to do that. Each child has his or her own toys; that is the way they learn to be responsible for themselves."

"What a barbaric country!" said Aunt Dua, "but listen to my son now, Grandma, because I think we really live in a good country."

Dua's son said, "You will love our country, Grandma. Our people treat everybody as equal. All have the same rights, nobody has special privileges. Nobody is very rich, and nobody is very poor. We elect our leaders, and the leaders walk the streets like everybody else. You can go up to them and talk with them. If most people think that a leader is not effective anymore, the leader will step back and the people will elect someone else."

"It sounds like you have weak leaders," said Aunt Satu sharply. "That would be fine if all people were good. But what about bad people? I think people need strong leaders; otherwise they will misbehave."

"How do you educate young boys and girls in your country?" asked Aunt Tiga.

"In our schools, students and teachers treat one another like equals," Dua's son explained. "In class, students may speak up whenever they want to, and teachers expect it. Students take as much initiative in class as teachers do."

"Is there no respect in your country?" said Aunt Ampat, visibly shocked. "How can you maintain discipline this way? How will these students behave in their work when they have left school? And how do they behave to their parents at home?"

"Of course we have masters and servants and bosses and subordinates in our country," said Dua's son. "But a subordinate is not worth less than the boss, and if I disagree with my boss, I will tell him so. As far as our home life goes, we treat our parents like equals, and they discuss things with us as soon as we are big enough to understand, when we are two or three years old."

"Discussing with a child of two?" said Aunt Lima. "Now come on, nephew, aren't you joking? Is that parental love? We love our children and protect them and make them feel safe, but we do not discuss adult topics with them. But let's hear from Tiga's daughter about life in her country."

And Tiga's daughter said, "Come live with us, Grandma. In our country people care for others regardless of whether they are friends or strangers. If someone needs help, she will get it. If someone cannot provide for himself, the country provides for him. We feel responsible for everybody."

"Doesn't that make people lazy?" asked Aunt Dua. "What's the use of doing your best if the country will take care of you anyway?"

"I don't think so," said Tiga's daughter. "We expect people to do their best but not to try overly hard to be the best—or to believe themselves to be better than others. We think that small is beautiful, and we do not like people who make themselves important and assertive. As children we learn to be modest and unassuming."

"Even boys?" Aunt Satu sounded very surprised. "Caring for the weak and being modest is natural for girls. Girls should be soft; we also do the crying, don't we? Shouldn't boys learn to be tough and assertive and to fight?"

"Funny you would say that," said Tiga's daughter. "We don't make so much of a difference in educating boys or girls. We don't like any child to fight—girls or boys. And in our country boys may cry just as much as girls; their parents will comfort them in the same way. We believe it makes everybody happier."

"Do fathers also comfort children if they cry?" asked Aunt Lima. "Isn't that for you to do, Tiga?"

"They come to whoever is closest by," said Aunt Tiga, somewhat upset. "What is wrong with that? When the children were babies their father played with them just as much as I did. No, we do not make such a big thing about a person being a man or a woman. If my daughter wants to learn carpentry, she is free to do so. If my son wants to play with dolls, we will not stop him. Men and women wear the same clothes, go to the same places, and have the same rights and duties. Many of our leaders are women, and they are respected just as much as the men are."

"What a decadent country!" Aunt Ampat cried out. "My son will tell you what a good country I landed in, Grandma."

And Ampat's son began, "In our country we believe in order and self-discipline. There are clear rules that everybody has to respect. Some of the stories you told about your countries make me very nervous. What if our children won't learn how to behave?"

"Isn't the way you educate your children rigid and dogmatic, then?" said Aunt Dua.

"Isn't the way you educate your children wishy-washy?" countered Ampat's son. "Ours is a principled country, that is true. We like to know the Truth and to teach it to the children. We do not like people who do otherwise. Those who do not think or behave like we do pose a threat to our way of life."

"You seem to forget that you are different yourself; your mother came in as a foreigner. How did that go? How could a stranger ever

EXPLORING CULTURE

be accepted in your country?" Aunt Tiga looked very surprised.

"True, that was not easy," confessed Aunt Ampat. "I had to learn a lot of rules and to be very careful to behave like everybody else. But my husband helped me."

"And you, children—how were you accepted, your mother being foreign?" asked Aunt Tiga.

"No, we weren't automatically accepted, that is so" said Ampat's son, visibly uneasy. "Every now and then somebody embarrasses me and my sister for being different. But then we make an extra effort to be real children of the country."

"This is all very confusing," Grandma said. "Your countries are each so different. But I haven't heard from Lima's daughter yet. Maybe hers is a country that I will feel comfortable living in."

Lima's daughter said, "Dear Grandma, you will really like our country. At home I never saw anybody worrying about Truth with a big T. We value people for what they do. What we learned as children was to work hard, to be enterprising, to save, and to never give up. We set our sights on the future. If that means that we have to subordinate ourselves to others for a time, we see nothing wrong with that."

"Do your people always work and never have fun?" asked Aunt Dua. "If you keep working for a future that moves away forever, you will never enjoy yourself. Is that what life is about? Working for tomorrow is fine, but not if you forget today."

"Working can be fun," said Lima's daughter. "We also have holidays, and we celebrate weddings, but we don't spend more than we can afford. We like to lend to our friends, not to borrow from them. We don't buy things just to keep up with the neighbors."

"Your people must be stingy, calculating, and cold," said Aunt Ampat disapprovingly. "I wouldn't feel comfortable in a country like that."

There was a long silence, and the five sisters looked at their mother and their families and each other and felt very uneasy. They had really grown apart. None of the five countries would please the other sisters.

Grandma shook her head and said she did not know whom to choose. She didn't like any of the countries—not Satu's do-your-own-thing country, Dua's equal country, Tiga's caring country, Ampat's principled country, or Lima's enterprising country. In the following years, she moved from one daughter to the other, enjoying all her offspring—and even their countries.

Five Basic Problems of Society

This was a fairy tale and, as such, did not really happen, as everybody knows. Or did it? This fairy tale, like many others, is based on truths, if you only know how to interpret it.

The five grandchildren and their families are not ordinary people, but they represent groups of people. Our world has been populated by groups that split and split and split again. Some stayed where they were, but many moved in search of a better life. The groups that settled in different countries developed their own ways to live that were adapted to their circumstances: ways to feed themselves, to form communities, to defend themselves against danger, to bring up their children, to explain the mysteries of life, and to express joy and fear and love and anger. This took many generations, and the old taught these things to the young. And as we all know, this process has not stopped today.

These ways to live are called cultures. In the Introduction we defined *culture* as "that which distinguishes one group of people from another." There are an infinite number of ways to form a culture, and no culture is objectively better or worse, superior or inferior, to another. Cultures are adaptations of a people to the conditions of life. When these conditions change, as they have over the last centuries, cultures are put under pressure. Still, they resist change. Today we find different cultures not only on different continents, but also in different countries and even parts of countries. A culture can never be all things to all people; what is good to one observer may be bad to another. English has the expression "You cannot have your cake and eat it too." You cannot have one aspect of a culture that you like without having other aspects that you may not like so much.

If you were to compare a large number of cultures around the world, you would see that although each is different, they all meet the same five basic problems of social life. Each culture has developed its own answers to each problem. Through what they told about their countries, the five grandchildren in the fairy tale described these five basic problems.

You cannot have one aspect of a culture that you like without having other aspects that you may not like so much.

EXPLORING CULTURE

Identity

Satu's daughter described a culture in which every individual could pursue his or her own interests without having to consider others. Her aunts did not like this notion because they believed that one has to adapt to others, especially relatives and friends. They believed that the groups to which one belongs determine who one is. In their view a person should be loyal to these groups, so that the groups will return the loyalty in times of need. Also, a person should always maintain harmony with the other group members.

The basic problem involved here is identity, the relationship between the individual and the group, and it can be seen as a spectrum ranging from individual identity, or *Individualism*, to group identity, or *Collectivism*. Satu's daughter described a very individualistic culture. The others preferred a more collectivist one.

The cultures of most wealthy countries in the world are relatively individualistic, and those of the poorer countries are relatively collectivistic. This is also historically true; as countries have become richer, they have also moved toward the individualist end of the spectrum. Collectivism can be seen as an adaptation to poverty and limited resources, and individualism, to wealth and ample resources. Wealth makes it easier for people to take care of themselves, to make it on their own. Yet a balance between the individual and others is always needed. In collectivist societies, individuals may have to repress their individual identities, and this may prove problematic. In very individualist societies, people may feel lonely and isolated, develop antisocial behaviors, or cling to illusions of group cohesion.

The issue of identity is crucial and far-reaching, and it has implications for many aspects of communication. Authorities on culture have called different manifestations of the same continuum by various names: individualist/collectivist, low-context/high-context, universalist/particularist, specific/diffuse, internal/external control, monochronic/polychronic cultures. This vari-

Collectivism can be seen as an adaptation to poverty and limited resources, and individualism, to wealth and ample resources.

ety has arisen because many interculturalists have found the identity continuum to be important. It shows how multifaceted this basic social issue is.

Hierarchy

The second basic issue is hierarchy, the degree of inequality between the people that is assumed to be a natural state of affairs. This attribute has been called *Power Distance*. Dua's son described a culture in which people were supposed to be equal, where the power distance was small. In such a society, it is still true that some people are better leaders than others are, but they will not make a show of their skills. Dua's aunts didn't like this idea either, because they wanted strong leaders to cope with bad people, and they believed in respect for teachers and parents. These attributes are associated with a larger power distance. In a society of large power distance, nobody thinks that people are all equal (or even should be) or should have the same prerogatives. Parents are not children, leaders are not followers, and kings are not citizens.

Many researchers have measured the degree of power distance in different countries. Such a measurement is always relative—one compares one country with other countries, just like the sisters did. And it depends on whom you consider, because power distance also differs within countries, becoming smaller as one climbs the social ladder. Within Europe, several studies have revealed that power distance in Northern and Western European cultures is smaller than in countries in Eastern and Southern Europe. The two areas are separated, roughly speaking and not coincidentally, by the former boundary of the Roman Empire. A similar line separates Anglo American from Latin American countries.

Hierarchy is related to wealth but not as strongly as identity is. Researchers have found that as a country has become wealthier, power distance has decreased in many cases. Large power distance is easier to maintain in a situation of poverty and limited resources.

Large power distance is easier to maintain in a situation of poverty and limited resources.

EXPLORING CULTURE

Gender

Tiga's daughter described a culture in which caring for others and being modest were important. Small was beautiful, better than achieving something big and being assertive. In her culture there was little difference between the education of boys and girls, and between the roles of mothers and fathers. Men and women wore the same clothes, went to the same places, and had the same rights and duties. Her aunts clearly preferred a more distinct role distribution between men and women. Men, they said, should be tougher than women.

The basic problem here centers on gender roles and the control of aggression. It has been found that in all countries in the world, an unequal role distribution between men and women coincides with a tougher society in which there is more emphasis on achievement and fighting than on caring and compromise. If men and women are more equal, the result is more "feminine" qualities within society as a whole. This is the reason why we call an equal role distribution between the genders in a culture *Feminine* and an unequal distribution, *Masculine*. Alternative names are care-oriented versus achievement-oriented. These names have the advantage of not being confused with *male* versus *female*, but they are less vivid.

Tiga's daughter described a very feminine culture, whereas her aunts preferred a masculine one. Big differences exist on this continuum even among countries in the same part of the world. For example, the cultures of the Netherlands and the Scandinavian countries are very feminine, but those of Germany, Switzerland, and Austria are strongly masculine; Costa Rica and Portugal are feminine, but Colombia and most other Latin American countries are masculine; Thailand is feminine, but Japan is very masculine. Britain and the United States are also rather masculine.

An unequal role distribution between men and women coincides with a tougher society in which there is more emphasis on achievement and fighting than on caring and compromise.

Truth

Ampat's son described a culture where people believed strongly in order and self-discipline, where there were clear rules and

The basic problem is how people in a culture cope with the unpredictable and the ambiguous. It has to do with anxiety as a basic human feeling, or in other words with fear of the unknown.

Truth with a capital *T*. This kind of culture was not very friendly to strangers. His aunts thought this culture rigid and dogmatic and preferred greater tolerance for differences. The basic problem is how people in a culture cope with the unpredictable and the ambiguous. It has to do with anxiety as a basic human feeling, or in other words with fear of the unknown. Many people in this kind of a culture believe that what is different is dangerous. This aspect of a culture has been called *Uncertainty Avoidance* as opposed to *Uncertainty Tolerance*. Anxiety and the search for Truth are closely related. Another name for this continuum would be one-truth orientation as opposed to many-truths orientation, but these labels are rather unwieldy, so we shall stick to the familiar label.*

Ampat landed in a culture that strongly avoided uncertainty, and she and her family had learned to feel comfortable in it. Her sisters preferred more tolerance of differences. Incidentally, uncertainty avoidance is not at all the same as risk avoidance; if risk can be acknowledged and quantified, it is not threatening to people from uncertainty avoiding cultures.

Russia and the countries of the Balkans have cultures of strong uncertainty avoidance, as do Japan, Korea, Mexico, Belgium, and France. Germanic countries are very uncomfortable with uncertainty. English-speaking countries and China tend to be more uncertainty tolerant. Singapore, Jamaica, and Denmark are very uncertainty tolerant.

Virtue

Lima's daughter described a culture in which hard work and persistence were important virtues, and children were taught to sacrifice the pleasures of today for the benefit of their future. Her aunts did not like this kind of country; one called it stingy, calculating, and cold. After all, one who saves for later cannot afford to buy presents and meals for friends today.

---

* Other authors have termed this continuum tight (strong uncertainty avoidance) as opposed to loose (weak uncertainty avoidance).

The basic problem is the choice between future and present virtue; this aspect of a culture is called *Long-Term Orientation* as opposed to *Short-Term Orientation*. The issue of virtue is particularly important in Asia and explains why non-Asians find it hard to come to grips with this cultural concept. Where Europeans and Americans are more concerned with truth, Asians are more concerned with virtue. Thus, to some extent the issues of truth and virtue are complementary in societies. Both are related to a society's attitude toward time and traditions.

Many countries of East Asia, like China and Japan, are considered to be long-term oriented, but some are not, for example, the Philippines. Most European and American countries are fairly short-term oriented. The Dutch, with a reputation in Europe for stinginess, are long-term oriented by European standards. African countries and Pakistan are very short-term oriented.

Summing Up

All people are alike in a way because they are biologically of the same species. All people are also unique individuals, and each person is unlike anyone else in the world. Third, all people are also social beings, and from early infancy on, they are taught how to survive in a social world. This involves coping with the five big issues we have just introduced: identity, hierarchy, gender, truth, and virtue. The way in which a group of people resolves these five issues is what we call culture. The world of a child in each culture is filled with symbols, heroes, and rituals that together embody and re-create that culture. Behind these manifestations are the values of the culture, about which the five grandchildren talked to their grandmother and their aunts in the fairy tale. Because these values are taught from birth, they manifest themselves in similar ways across social settings: family, school, workplace, and others. Likewise, they hold for all ages, both genders, and all professions, and they define the roles of these different entities in society.

The issue of virtue is particularly important in Asia and explains why non-Asians find it hard to come to grips with this cultural concept.

These cultural values can range from high to low on five *dimensions of culture* that correspond to the five issues. Each dimension spans a continuum from one extreme position to the other regarding that particular social issue. The opposite poles of each dimension are named according to the terms introduced within each value above.

Value Dimensions

Dimension	One Extreme	Other Extreme
Identity	Collectivism	Individualism
Hierarchy	Large Power Distance	Small Power Distance
Gender	Femininity	Masculinity
Truth	Strong Uncertainty Avoidance	Weak Uncertainty Avoidance
Virtue	Long-Term Orientation	Short-Term Orientation

Major Aspects of Culture

Culture Is Problematic

We have now introduced you to a widely accepted definition of national culture and given you a template for studying the values of these cultures. There are, however, still numerous problematic aspects about culture.

- Culture is not a universally accepted notion, and there are a great many different ways to define it. However, all but the most exotic definitions include, as we do, the sense that culture pertains to the social world; it determines how groups of people structure their lives.

- Once you begin considering culture, there is the problem of knowing where to stop. Do you include all value-related sources such as demographics, status levels, affiliations, and identities, or do you limit yourself to one or two categories? In this book, empirical data on national cultures are a starting point. National cultures constitute the social fabric in which each individual has a place. Ethnic or regional subcultures can function in a way that is analogous to national culture, but they do not usually have school systems, legal systems, and other social institutions that nations employ to reinforce their dominant value systems. Professional, corporate, or age-related subcultures are usually no more than variations in the fabric of national culture. These subcultural groups can have their own heroes, symbols, and rituals, but they share the values of the national culture in which they operate.

- There is also the question of who decides what the rules are for any given culture and who is the legitimate interpreter of those rules. Of course, these rules are emergent in social interaction, they are forever reinventing and reinterpreting themselves, and the final word on them can never be said.

- Culture only manifests itself through social action that always takes place in a changing context. For instance, political events or technological advances can drastically change the context in which people live. A change in context does not, however, in itself constitute a change in culture, though it puts pressure on culture. The effects of culture and context are not easily separable. It is easy to misinterpret a context effect for a culture effect, or vice versa. One can see culture's consequences everywhere or nowhere.

Culture only manifests itself through social action that always takes place in a changing context.

One can see culture's consequences everywhere or nowhere.

- Because culture is so complex and dynamic, problems of reliability and validity make it very difficult to measure.

- Perhaps most profoundly, persons who are members of a culture may not be able to describe that culture accurately and articulately in a way that would be accepted by another person who is also a member of the same culture, or understood by a person who is not a member of that culture. Value systems are implicit, and values defy conscious reflection.

To sum up, the social nature of culture makes it a somewhat elusive phenomenon.

In any intercultural encounter, there is always a temptation to feel that the others have bad character or bad intentions, rather than to realize that they are acting according to different rules.

When people are interacting with each other across cultures, their cultural values could make them say or do things that are misperceived as intentional.

Culture Is Not Personality

It is not always easy to disentangle personal behavior from cultural characteristics. In any intercultural encounter, there is always a temptation to feel that the others have bad character or bad intentions, rather than to realize that they are acting according to different rules.

People from individualist cultures may attribute culture-based behavior to personal character even more readily, because they are less likely to perceive the invisible hand of the group. They do not like to be categorized in a group, as if they were not unique individuals. They have a hard time seeing that they are both unique individuals and share a common culture with their fellow countrymen and –women. People from collectivist cultures may make the opposite error: they attribute behavior of individuals to a group intention. We saw this happen in The Frankfurt Incident, where the collectivist North Koreans thought that the United States was behind the humiliating treatment inflicted on their delegation, not merely some security personnel from an airline company.

When people are interacting with each other across cultures, their cultural values could make them say or do things that are misperceived as intentional. Some stereotypic kinds of misattribution exist across cultures as a result of differences along the culture dimensions. Let us give a much simplified overview of some of these.

In an apparent analogy to the dimensions of culture, psychology also distinguishes five dimensions: openness, conscientiousness, extraversion, agreeableness, and neuroticism. This is not the place to discuss these "big five" personality dimensions, but only to caution the reader to be aware of the distinction. The five dimensions from psychology are entirely different concepts from the five dimensions of national culture.

Misattributions of Culture-Based Behaviors

Listener who is culturally more...	...can misperceive culture-based behavior of foreigners as...
Collectivist	insulting, stressed, heartless, rude
Individualist	dishonest, corrupt
Large Power Distance Oriented	disrespectful, improper, rude
Small Power Distance Oriented	bossy, rigid (of high-status persons); servile, cowardly (of low-status persons)
Feminine	aggressive, showing off (of men); playing "baby doll" (of women)
Masculine	weak (of men); unfeminine (of women)
Strong Uncertainty Avoiding	unprincipled, amoral
Weak Uncertainty Avoiding	rigid, paranoid
Long-term Oriented	irresponsible, throwing away money
Short-term Oriented	stingy, cold

Culture Differences and Language Differences

One could wonder whether differences in national culture have anything to do with language differences. We know that each language has its own vocabulary and style, and it is very hard to translate books without losing the finer nuances of meaning. This is understandable. Every language has evolved along with the society using it, so language differences between countries usually point to differences in culture. The reverse is not always true, however. It turns out that having the same language does not necessarily mean sharing the same culture. Two countries can differ greatly in culture even though their people speak the same language. Take, for example, the case of the Netherlands and Vlaanderen (Flanders), the neighboring northern part of Belgium. The two countries share a common, open border and a common language, though differing in dia-

Two countries can differ greatly in culture even though their people speak the same language.

lect; yet their national cultures are quite different and have been so for many centuries. The historical reason can be traced to the Roman Empire.

Although the dimensions of national culture are independent of one another, some of them occur together in clusters of countries. This is notably so in Europe, where the southern countries are characterized by larger power distance, higher masculinity, and stronger uncertainty avoidance than are the northern ones. The boundary between these groups of countries more or less follows the former delimitation of the Roman Empire. The contrast between Belgium and the Netherlands is a case in point, because Belgium has a Latin culture, influenced by the Roman Empire, whereas the Netherlands was hardly affected by the Romans at all. Here is an account by a Dutchman working in Belgium for a Dutch cleaning company.

Rules in the Cleaning Company

During my work as a regional management assistant at a firm providing cleaning services in Belgium, I came into contact with a lot of people. Because I had to make new cleaning schedules and cost calculations for new and old customers, I met all the employees, both at headquarters and the operating core working at different sites.

The first thing I noticed was the relationship between a superior and a subordinate. Orders from a superior were to be obeyed, not questioned. Informal relations between people from different positions in the hierarchy were minimal; for example, no secretary had lunch with her boss. Subordinates expected superiors to tell them what to do. When I talked to the people on the work floor, they always called me Mr. so-and-so, although I had told them my first name. They also expected me to tell them what to do, even if they had more experience in their areas than I did. This was difficult for me in the beginning. Sometimes people stared at me in surprise when I did something they did not expect, for example, when I helped carry some cleaning ma-terials, which in their eyes was inappropriate. Some Belgians appreciated this no-nonsense style, but it also created some confusion.

The Belgians were used to following the rules, and when rules were absent, they wanted a direct and clear decision or order from their superior. The work schedules and job descriptions had to be very detailed. If something went wrong, the employees often referred to their job descriptions and their work schedules and said that according to these, they hadn't done anything wrong. Sorting through such tangles took a lot of my management time. Sometimes it was as if we talked a different language.

The kind of job one had was also very important. To the Belgians, a good job meant high esteem in society. Almost everyone was trying to improve his or her position or at least make it look more important. Also, money was very important. Not only did the money one earned tell something about the job one had, but this money also made it possible to buy a large and beautiful house and a big car.

Three dimensions of culture are involved in this story: power distance, uncertainty avoidance, and masculinity. First, differences in power distance are manifest in this young manager's account. Belgium has a larger power distance than the Netherlands does. Compared with the Dutch, the Belgians were used to a steep hierarchy and a stratified social life. Second, the two countries are wide apart on the scale of uncertainty avoidance. Belgium has a stronger uncertainty avoidance than the Netherlands. To the Dutchman, the Belgians appeared obsessed with detailed instructions. Finally, there is a considerable difference in masculinity between the Belgians and the Dutch. The Belgian culture is more masculine. The Dutchman perceived the Belgians as wanting to make themselves look better.

The seeming ease of contact that a common language provided hid a marked difference in organizational practices. The Dutchman's remark, "Sometimes it was as if we talked a different language," held some truth; the words may have meant the same in the two countries, but they did not come across in the same way, because the rules about who was supposed to talk to whom and about what were different.

Awareness of Culture Differences

We shall now revisit each of the five basic dimensions of culture through ten true stories. Although in real life culture never manifests itself as purely one-dimensional, each of the stories does highlight how one or more of the basic issues in particular can cause problems in intercultural encounters. Each of the stories in the following exercise appears in two versions: a "working" version and a "highlighted" version. The exercise tests your ability to recognize cultural differences as portrayed in the stories, based on what you have learned so far about the five dimensions of culture (see pages 35–39).

The Wedding Guest

An American was hired as an external consultant to assess the progress of a development project in Indonesia. The consultant already suspected from other sources that the project was in trouble due to mismanagement by the Northern European project leader. This opinion was confirmed to him by an Indonesian engineer, albeit in a reluctant manner. From the Indonesian's veiled account, the consultant deduced that the project leader was in fact an utter failure. The consultant then asked the Indonesian whether he had told the project leader that he was not doing well. "That is not so," said the Indonesian. "Why not?" asked the consultant. The Indonesian engineer replied, "He was a guest at my wedding."

See if you can determine which words and phrases indicate cultural differences between the American and the Indonesian. When you have done this, underline them. Then read on and find out which words and phrases we chose to highlight in the version below. A discussion of our interpretation follows, which identifies the concept(s), analyzes the situation, and provides the contextual meaning.

An American was hired as an **external consultant** to assess the progress of a development project in Indonesia. The consultant already suspected from other sources that the project was in trouble due to mismanagement by the Northern European project leader. This opinion was confirmed to him by an Indonesian engineer, albeit **in a reluctant manner**. From the Indonesian's **veiled account**, the consultant deduced that the project leader was in fact **an utter failure**. The consultant then asked the Indonesian **whether he had told** the project leader that he was not doing well. **"That is not so,"** said the Indonesian. **"Why not?"** asked the consultant. The Indonesian engineer replied, **"He was a guest at my wedding."**

Discussion: Identity

Spot the concept: In this account the differences between a collectivist "insider" and an individualist "outsider" perspective are clear and important.

Analysis: The company insiders held the collectivist value of protecting one another against threats from the outside. In a collectivistic value system, external auditing is not desirable. The external consultant became a threat to the local European manager, who had gained insider status as indicated by being invited to the wedding of the project leader. Although the local manager and the external consultant were both foreigners, they were evaluated differently; the local manager had been accepted as "belonging" and therefore required—and received—the protection of the others against any external threat. The difference along the individualism-collectivism continuum is also apparent in the direct questioning by the American, as opposed to the Indonesian's indirect style.

Meaning: Rather than identify the problem as being mismanagement by one individual group member (the European manager), the task ahead is more one of restoring harmony within the collectivity of the local company. One solution would be to retrain the local European manager to do a better job, thereby preserving his role in the group. If the European manager is punished, then the entire collective group may perceive this as a punishment of itself as well and respond accordingly, whatever the intention of the external consultant. If, however, it becomes necessary to remove the local European manager, an outsider, such as the external consultant, would be the best choice for the unpleasant task. After all, he will probably never "be invited to the project manager's wedding," so to speak, and will never become an insider. It would be very difficult and perhaps impossible for the other insiders to exclude the local European manager, no matter how much of a failure he might be.

The difference along the individualism-collectivisim continuum is also apparent in the direct questioning by the American, as opposed to the Indonesian's indirect style.

EXPLORING CULTURE

Rebecca Dooley, an American consultant, recounts an experience she had:

The Job Candidate

I was traveling from London to Amsterdam on a consultancy assignment for a U.S. high-tech company. Accompanying me was the head of HR for all European operations, who was Irish and who had been in his position for sixteen years. We got onto the subject of understanding and doing business with different cultures, when he suddenly leaned over and said earnestly in his Irish lilt, "Whatever you do, you don't want to be doing business with the Dutch!" I asked him why not, and he proceeded to explain.

"I very nearly hired a Dutch fellow to become a director of marketing. He had all the right skills, experience, and references and had impressed all the other directors of the region during our multiple-interview process. Just as we were in the final stages of hiring him, he asked if it would be possible to work forty-eight hours per week, within four days of the week. I was aghast and told him that this would be inconceivable. You can believe I quickly ended the hiring process then and there. I realized it would be impossible to get the kind of total commitment to the company from him we expected, with that kind of attitude.

He was only thirty-three years old, for goodness sakes. What would such a young man do with three days off?! Not only that, but whenever I've negotiated an opportunity with a potential Dutch candidate, they always have to go home first and talk everything over with their wives and family before giving an answer. With me, I make the business decisions and inform my wife. She trusts my judgment to be in the best interest for all of us. Not in Holland! The wives have the power to veto any opportunity at any time. I tell you it's the women who wear the pants around there! The point is that with all this going on, you'll never get anything done if you work with the Dutch!"

As we were landing and admiring the ingenuity and organization of the tulip beds and greenhouses stretching for miles and miles below us, I commented that they certainly seemed to accomplish quite a lot anyway. Later, in the Amsterdam office, I observed that of the management population at that site, indeed only one was Dutch. Unfortunately, I was unable to meet him because he was on extended holiday.

Can you find the phrases and sentences that are culturally significant? Again, underline those phrases and then read our version with the significant text highlighted.

I was traveling from London to Amsterdam on a consultancy assignment for a U.S. high-tech company. Accompanying me was the head of HR for all European operations, who was Irish and who had been in his position for sixteen years. We got onto the subject of understanding and doing business with different cultures, when he suddenly leaned over and said earnestly in his Irish lilt, "Whatever you do, **you don't want to be doing business with the Dutch!**" I asked him why not, and he proceeded to explain.

"I very nearly hired a Dutch fellow to become a director of marketing. He had all the right skills, experience, and references and had impressed all the other directors of the region during our multiple-interview process. Just as we were in the final stages of hiring him, he asked if it would be possible to work **forty-eight hours** per week, within **four days** of the week. I was **aghast** and told him that this would be **inconceivable**. You can believe I quickly ended the hiring process then and there. I realized it would be impossible to get the kind of **total commitment to the company** from him we expected, with that kind of attitude.

He was only thirty-three years old, for goodness sakes. **What would such a young man do with three days off**?! Not only that, but whenever I've negotiated an opportunity with a potential Dutch candidate, they always have to go home first and **talk everything over with their wives and family** before giving an answer. With me, **I make the business decisions and inform my wife. She trusts my judgment** to be in the best interest for all of us. Not in Holland! The wives have the power to veto any opportunity at any time. I tell you **it's the women who wear the pants around there!** The point is that with all this going on, **you'll never get anything done if you work with the Dutch!**"

As we were landing and admiring the ingenuity and organization of the tulip beds and greenhouses stretching for miles and miles below us, I commented that they certainly seemed to accomplish quite a lot anyway. Later, in the Amsterdam office, I observed that of the management population at that site, indeed only one was Dutch. Unfortunately, I was unable to meet him because he was on **extended holiday**.

Discussion: Gender

Spot the concept: Almost every sentence uttered by the Irish HR manager speaks of the typical kind of misunderstandings that occur between people from two countries that differ on the cultural dimension of masculinity; the Irish are masculine, whereas the Dutch are feminine.

Analysis: The Irishman did not interpret the Dutch applicant's request as culturally embedded. Instead he used his own frame of reference to interpret it and concluded that the candidate was not committed to the job. That led him to discard an excellent candidate.

Meaning: It is possible for two culturally different people to disagree about their behavior without either one being "wrong" as long as they can agree on the common-ground objectives or shared goals. When behaviors are interpreted outside their cultural context, those behaviors are usually inaccurately interpreted, resulting in misunderstanding and inappropriate intervention. The Dutch are very industrious while on the job but value their private time; the primary social distinction is home versus work, not men's world versus women's. Actually, four-day management jobs are not common in Holland, but they do occur, and the economy seems none the worse for it. As for this particular firm, with such a hiring policy in place for sixteen years, it is no wonder that there were hardly any Dutch managers to be found. This shows how the hiring process can make corporate culture follow national culture, even in multinational firms.

When behaviors are interpreted outside their cultural context, those behaviors are usually inaccurately interpreted, resulting in misunderstanding and inappropriate intervention.

Here is the story of a young Dutchman, five years after the event.

Extreme Hospitality

When I was fifteen years old, I played indoor soccer. I was a member of a very nice team; we were friends. Once we played Maluku, our biggest rival. Maluku is an association for people from the Maluku Islands in Indonesia, many of whom live in Holland. After the game, which we lost 5 to 1, we were invited to the canteen (bar) of the Maluku Club. Whole families were present there. They insisted we join in and eat and drink with them. I felt very uneasy. They were all relaxed and friendly and really pleased to be with us, but somehow I was very frightened by their extreme hospitality. After having been there for a short time, I stood up and went to the toilet, and I stayed there for half an hour. I was just washing my hands when the coach of the Maluku team came in. He asked me where I had been for so long, and I told him that I had been in the rest room be- cause I had a terrible stomachache. When we reached the canteen again, there was a loud and happy party going on. Although I didn't want to hurt my hosts' feelings, I just couldn't go back in there. I told the coach of the Maluku team that I still felt bad and asked him to leave me alone for a minute. After the coach had joined the party again, I took my bag, ran out of the building, and went home.

The people of the Maluku Islands still think that I had a stomachache that night. If they knew I left because I felt frightened by their hospitality, I'm sure they would feel very sad about it. I'm almost sure they would think I did not like them, but I do. I have been in similar situations since then, and I have experienced the joy and warmth these people are able to share so easily. Back then, though, it was new and somehow unreal to me.

Please read the story again and underline the phrases that you think indicate culture differences. When you have done that, compare your version with our interpretation of significant phrases below.

When I was fifteen years old, I played indoor soccer. I was a member of a very nice team; **we were friends**. Once we played Maluku, our biggest rival. Maluku is an association for people from the Maluku Islands in Indonesia, many of whom live in Holland. After the game, which we lost 5 to 1, **we were invited** to the canteen (bar) of the Maluku Club. **Whole families were present there. They insisted we join in** and eat and drink with them. **I felt very uneasy.** They were all relaxed and friendly and really pleased to be with us, but somehow **I was very frightened by their extreme hospitality**. After having been there for a short time, I stood up and went to the toilet, and I stayed there for half an hour. I was just washing my hands when the coach of the Maluku team came in. He asked me where I had been for so long, and I told him that I had been in the rest room because I had a **terrible stomachache**. When we reached the canteen again, there was a loud and **happy party** going on. Although I didn't want to hurt my hosts' feelings, I just **couldn't go back in there**. I told the coach of the Maluku team that I still felt bad and asked him **to leave me alone** for a minute. After the coach had joined the party, **I took my bag, ran out of the building**, and went home.

The people of the Maluku Islands still think that I had a stomachache that night. If they knew I left because I felt frightened by their hospitality, I'm sure they would feel very sad about it. I'm almost sure they would think I did not like them, but I do. I have been in similar situations since then, and I have experienced **the joy and warmth these people are able to share so easily**. Back then, though, it was new and **somehow unreal to me**.

Discussion: Identity

Spot the concept: In this story, individual versus group identity is at stake, as shown by the boldface (highlighted) text.

Analysis: The Maluku team held collectivist values. In line with those values, they considered their rival team to be guests of honor and therefore "part of the family." The Dutch boys, on the other hand, were individualists, and they were not used to being so close and exuberant, not even with one another. Note that the boy makes no mention whatsoever of his team members in the later part of his account. He speaks of "I," not "we," and he wants to be left alone. Caught between his fear of joining the party and of offending his hosts, the boy pleaded physical illness. In most cultures this is an acceptable excuse for not following the local rules.

Meaning: It is significant that this event is still important to the Dutchman, even five years after it took place. An important clash of cultures occurred from which he is still learning five years later. He is now able to better understand the collectivist Maluku culture and is better able to adapt his social behavior to a similar cultural setting.

By the way, the importance of losing is interpreted differently by each culture. Had the boy been from a masculine culture, then his team might not have been keen to celebrate with their victors. But in a feminine culture such as the Dutch, losing is not a big deal, and it would not have made any difference to the story if the boy's team had won 5-1.

Half a Greek

A multinational company had manufacturing facilities in Greece. The U.S. headquarters appointed Nick Nikopoulos, born in the United States like his parents but with Greek ancestry, as a floor manager. His assignment was to improve efficiency without firing people. Nick was anxious to get ahead. He thought he would start by establishing a good working relationship with the existing workers. His first action was to call in his direct reports, the shift leaders, for a meeting. He told them in his broken Greek, "I want to launch an efficiency operation. Since you have worked here longer than I have, I would like to ask your opinion about the optimal duration of a number of tasks."

To his surprise and discomfort, the shift leaders stared at the floor mutely, until one of the older ones finally said, "Sir, you are the boss. Why don't you just tell us what to do?" Nick began to realize that he was not as Greek as he had thought he was back in the U.S.

Now reread the story and underline the phrases that point to culture differences. When you have done this, read on and find out how we have interpreted the incident.

A multinational company had manufacturing facilities in Greece. The U.S. headquarters appointed Nick Nikopoulos, born in the United States but with Greek ancestry, as a floor manager. His assignment was to improve efficiency without firing people. Nick was **anxious to get ahead**. He thought he would start by establishing a **good working relationship** with the existing workers. His first action was to call in his direct reports, the shift leaders, for a meeting. He told them in his broken Greek, "I want to launch an efficiency operation. Since you have worked here longer than I have, **I would like to ask your opinion** about the optimal duration of a number of tasks."

To his surprise and discomfort, the shift leaders **stared at the floor mutely**, until **one of the older ones** finally said, "Sir, **you are the boss**. Why don't **you just tell us** what to do?" Nick began to realize that he was not as Greek as he had thought he was back in the U.S.

Discussion: Hierarchy

Spot the concept: The text in boldface type indicates that Nick comes from a culture low on power distance, whereas his shift leaders are used to large power distance.

Analysis: Calling in his inferiors or wanting to change things was not problematic. Misunderstandings arose when Nick asked his direct reports for their opinions. From their perspective this was a sign of weak leadership. But the same issue, large power distance, made them reluctant to say this to Nick's face. If Nick had first made a speech showing firmness and a sense of purpose, he might have asked his question afterward with more success.

Meaning: Nick took it for granted that he could apply his usual U.S. approach with his Greek shift leaders. He was of Greek ancestry, after all, and spoke the language. But he recognized a bit too late that this was not sufficient. With reflection and practice, he will acquire a bicultural identity, with the ability to move from the American to the Greek perspective and back again. This will enable him to increase efficiency while at the same time preserving the large power distance preferences of his staff.

George Bush in Japan

In 1991 the American president George Bush Sr. traveled to Japan for a trade mission. He was accompanied by several of the leading business tycoons from the United States. Their mission was to discuss trade regulations. What they really wanted was to curb Japanese competition. They complained that the Japanese were flooding the U.S. with products while keeping their own borders closed to American products, which was causing layoffs back home.

The Japanese were not impressed. They pointed to the fact that an American CEO earns about two million dollars per year, which is six times as much as a Japanese CEO makes, while the Japanese pay more taxes. This money should go into the business, they said. In Japan, they explained, when the business takes a downturn, the CEO cuts his own salary before laying anybody off. If these American CEOs cared more about the future of their companies and less about their own bank accounts, the Japanese said, their business problems would be solved. Obviously, the trade dispute was not settled. Incidentally, quite a few Americans openly agreed with the Japanese line of reasoning, among whom was Bill Clinton, the ambitious governor of Arkansas who wanted to run for president.

Read the story and underline significant words and phrases. Then read our version.

In 1991 the American president George Bush Sr. traveled to Japan for a trade mission. He was accompanied by several of the **leading business tycoons** from the United States. Their mission was to discuss trade regulations. What they really wanted was to **curb Japanese competition**. They complained that the Japanese were flooding the U.S. with products while keeping their own borders closed to American products, which was causing layoffs back home.

The Japanese were not impressed. They pointed to the fact that an American CEO earns about two million dollars per year, which is **six times as much as a Japanese** CEO makes, while the **Japanese pay more taxes**. This money should go into the business, they said. In Japan, they explained, when the business takes a downturn, the **CEO cuts his own salary before laying anybody off**. If these **American CEOs cared more about the future of their companies** and **less about their own bank accounts**, the Japanese said, their business problems would be solved. Obviously, the trade dispute was not settled. Incidentally, quite a few Americans openly agreed with the Japanese line of reasoning, among whom was Bill Clinton, the ambitious governor of Arkansas who wanted to run for president.

Discussion: Virtue and Identity

Spot the concept: The response of the Japanese addressed both the short-term orientation and the individualism of the Americans, as indicated by the words and phrases in boldface.

Analysis: The "big picture" was more important to the Japanese businessmen than to the Americans. The Japanese emphasized the longer-term outcomes of the business and its collective welfare. The Americans were more focused on scoring a point by changing trade and tariff arrangements. They intended to impress the Japanese by bringing some of their most powerful, super-rich businessmen. In the United States, these tycoons are cultural heroes and command great respect. The Japanese struck back by attacking what they perceived to be unethical personal enrichment by the American CEOs. What began as a discussion of trade rules ended up with two very different social systems criticizing one another. Consequently, not only were the specific trading rules left in dispute but now the conflict had also escalated considerably, making future discussions even more difficult. Incidentally, because both the U.S. and Japan are masculine cultures, fighting in itself is seen as a proper way of dealing with disagreements by both parties and may even have contributed to mutual respect, if not to an agreement.

Meaning: There is a significant difference between individualist cultures that put emphasis on short-term context, such as Anglo cultures, and collectivist cultures that emphasize long-term context, such as the Japanese. In order to reach an agreement between these two positions, it is more fruitful for both sides to consider the long-term context in which decisions are made. It is not coincidence that Asians have sayings of the type, "If you keep an American waiting long enough, he'll sign anything." If they had put more emphasis on the long-term

There is a significant difference between individualist cultures that put emphasis on short-term context, such as Anglo cultures, and collectivist cultures that emphasize long-term context, such as the Japanese.

outcomes, the Americans would not have given up any bargaining power while the Japanese would have felt much better understood. The Japanese, on the other hand, would have had a very difficult time disregarding the long-term context and implications of their immediate decisions.

This is the story of Fernando, a young man from Spain.

Fernando and the Napkin

Two years ago I lived with an Irish family for fifteen days during the summer. The first day when I sat at the table to have lunch, I realized that there was no napkin beside my plate. I asked the Irish woman for one, and she reacted as if I had asked for the strangest thing in the world. I felt bad because I thought that they thought I was a dirty boy who needed a napkin to clean what I was going to soil. However, I was sure that my behavior was correct. Afterward, she took a napkin and gave it to me, and for the remaining days she did the same not only for me but also for the rest of the family.

Please underline the culturally significant words or phrases. Then compare your choices with our version.

Two years ago I lived with an Irish family for fifteen days during the summer. The first day when I sat at the table to have lunch, I realized that there was **no napkin beside my plate**. I asked the Irish woman for one, and she reacted as if I had asked for the **strangest thing in the world. I felt bad** because I thought that they thought I was a **dirty boy** who needed a napkin **to clean what I was going to soil**. However, I was **sure that my behavior was correct.** Afterward, she took a napkin and gave it to me, and for the remaining days she did the same not only for me but **also for the rest of the family**.

Discussion: Truth

Spot the concept: The misunderstanding focuses on uncertainty avoidance. The young man from Spain is used to fixed symbols and rituals, as highlighted by the boldface type, whereas the Irish family seems more casual.

Analysis: The napkin came to symbolize the structure and order to which the young man from Spain was accustomed. In response to hearing Fernando's preference, the Irish mother generously provided him with a napkin. Although Fernando initially took the woman's response as an insult, he probably reinterpreted her response the next day when she also provided everyone else with a napkin, showing that he was not being singled out as a dirty boy. The response by the Irish family members was both insightful and generous. They may have talked about his dismay among themselves after the first meal and decided to all use napkins during the remainder of Fernando's stay. They did not condemn the young man for his request or his discomfort; instead, they adapted their own behavior to accommodate him.

Meaning: Culture is communicated through symbols. Some of these are as ordinary as a napkin. However, even ordinary symbols can have a powerful influence on relationships and the ultimate success or failure of an encounter. In this case the young man's expectations that meals include napkins were met, and by providing napkins for everyone else as well, the host mother validated the young man's preference. Uncertainty avoiding cultures have rigid rules about cleanliness. Once the host family understood the young man's need for structure, it was able to accommodate his preferences without compromising the integrity of its own preference for a more informal style. This is typical of contacts between people from uncertainty avoiding cultures and uncertainty tolerant ones: those from uncertainty tolerant ones are more likely to adapt.

Culture is communicated through symbols. Some of these are as ordinary as a napkin. However, even ordinary symbols can have a powerful influence on relationships and the ultimate success or failure of an encounter.

This account is by a young woman from the Netherlands. Can you see what dimensions of national culture stand out?

In the Pub

I have observed German and Dutch boys in the pub at night. It strikes me every time that huge differences exist between the Dutch and Germans, who live so close to each other.

German boys just go out with boys. They go out with girls only when they happen to be their girlfriends. Also, going out in Germany is about discussing the problems of the world, like environment, war, politics, and economics. Choose any subject, and they will be happy to discuss it. Germans talk a lot about their ideals and opinions. In discussions between German and Dutch students, I have observed a lot of misunderstandings because the Germans were only talking about ideals, while the Dutch were talking about what could be done to overcome present difficulties. Germans have the habit of judging each other. They have heated discussions about being right or wrong in conversations. The Dutch have discussions, too, but they are not very serious most of the time. They ask for others' opinions and try to reach a compromise, and they are reluctant to give their own opinions strongly.

The German turn-taking behavior in discussions is also very different. Dutch students listen to another person and give their comments afterward, in a more gentle form; they believe everybody is allowed to have his or her own opinion. German students interrupt each other, clearly disagree with what has been said, and try to convince other participants in the discussion of the mistakes in their arguments. I have also observed that Germans have the same personality everywhere; they will stick to one role, whereas the Dutch adapt their behavior to the situation.

Here is the same story, but with significant passages highlighted. Again, underline words and phrases indicating cultural misunderstandings, then read our version.

I have observed German and Dutch boys in the pub at night. It strikes me every time that huge differences exist between the Dutch and Germans, who live so close to each other.

German boys **just go out with boys**. They go out with girls **only when they happen to be their girlfriends**. Also, going out in Germany is about **discussing the problems of the world**, like environment, war, politics, and economics. Choose any subject, and they will be happy to discuss it. Germans talk a lot about their **ideals and opinions**. In discussions between German and Dutch students, I have observed a lot of misunderstandings because the Germans were only talking about ideals, while the **Dutch were talking about what could be done** to overcome present difficulties. Germans have the habit of **judging each other**. They have heated discussions about being right or wrong in conversations. The Dutch have discussions, too, but they are not very serious most of the time. They **ask for others' opinions and try to reach a compromise**, and they are **reluctant to give their own opinions strongly**.

The German turn-taking behavior in discussions is also very different. Dutch students listen to another person and give their comments **afterward**, in a **more gentle form**; they believe everybody is allowed to have his or her own opinion. German students **interrupt each other**, clearly **disagree** with what has been said, and **try to convince** other participants in the discussion of the mistakes in their arguments. I have also observed that Germans have the same personality everywhere; they will **stick to one role**, whereas the Dutch **adapt their behavior to the situation**.

Discussion: Truth and Gender

Spot the concept: In this account the key concepts for the German students are truth, clarity, right, and wrong. They want order in their opinions and in their private lives. The key notions for the Dutch students are compromise and adaptability, both in their opinions and in their lives. The underlying dimensions of culture are uncertainty avoidance and masculinity-femininity.

Analysis: Germans are somewhat higher on uncertainty avoidance than the Dutch. For the German students, finding the truth is a very important and desirable thing. In fact it is so important to them that they are willing to spend their night out trying to determine it. They do not think ill of interrupting each other in a discussion; in fact by interrupting they show that they are listening and involved. When they try to convince somebody of their own opinion, they are doing that person the honor of taking him or her seriously. They argue with some vehemence. In their lives they also try to get rid of ambiguity; they do not go into a pub with a girl if she is not clearly "the" girlfriend; they do not take on different roles in different situations. This moderate difference in uncertainty avoidance between the two countries is conspicuous for the Dutch storyteller because she is Dutch herself and perceives what is different.

The Dutch also have discussions, but in their case, the truth is less important than letting all the participants express their own opinions. Stressing one's point of view is not considered polite. The Dutch are more relaxed and pragmatic, with an eye on resolving conflicting interests. The considerable difference in masculinity accounts for the Germans' habit of "fighting a discussion out," compared with the Dutch tendency to compromise.

Meaning: The pub is not all that different from other situations in which the Dutch and Germans converse. In meetings, too, differences between the two cultures can occur. The Dutch may take offense if they are interrupted by Germans; they may feel that the Germans are not letting them finish talking, while in fact the Germans may just be trying to show a genuine interest by starting to argue. On the other hand, the Germans might take offense if the Dutch fail to counter their arguments and try to settle for compromises instead of yielding to the force of normative arguments.

This is another pub story by a Dutch girl.

Who Pays for the Drink?

Last summer some people from all over Europe came to the Netherlands to attend a language course in English. Among them was a Romanian boy, Septi, who was studying medicine. One night there was a party, and I offered Septi something to drink. He refused; instead he immediately went to buy me and himself a drink. Some time later I tried again, but he seemed to be uncomfortable about my paying for the drinks. A Dutch boy tried to offer him a drink, and after two refusals Septi finally accepted one drink from this boy but immediately bought another drink for the Dutch boy.

I found Septi's behavior very strange at the time. In the Netherlands, students and other young people normally offer a drink to someone they like. I had never had trouble, until that night, offering a boy a drink. It is normal among friends, as we earn about the same amount of money.

Follow the same procedure with this story as with the preceding ones.

Last summer some people from all over Europe came to the Netherlands to attend a language course in English. Among them was a Romanian boy, Septi, who was studying medicine. One night there was a party, and I offered Septi something to drink. **He refused; instead** *he* **immediately** *went to buy me and himself a drink. Some time later I tried again, but he seemed to be* **uncomfortable about my paying for** *the drinks. A Dutch boy tried to offer him a drink, and* **after two refusals Septi finally accepted** *one drink from this boy* **but immediately bought another drink** *for the Dutch boy.*

I found Septi's behavior very strange at the time. In the Netherlands, students and other young people normally offer a drink to **someone they like. I had never had trouble**, *until that night,* **offering a boy a drink**. *It is* **normal among friends**, *as we* **earn about the same amount of money**.

Discussion: Gender and Virtue

Spot the concept: For Septi, being offered a drink has a strong symbolic meaning that is linked with gender and with reciprocity. For the Dutch the meaning is different. You offer drinks to friends regardless of gender, taking into consideration whether you can afford it. The underlying dimensions of culture in this story are masculinity/femininity and short-term/long-term orientation.

Analysis: The storyteller's account also included an analysis that was so clear that we reproduce it here.

"Septi's masculine pride must have been at stake, not only because he was offered a drink by a girl, but also because he might have thought I only offered him these drinks because he was not as wealthy as I, a Westerner, am. Because he eventually accepted a drink from a boy, I guess the most important factor must have been refusing a drink offered by a girl. If I faced the same situation again, I would still offer a drink to a foreign boy. If he refused to accept it and if I thought he did not want to accept something from a girl, I would not offer again. If a friendship had deepened, he might have been able to accept me as I am and accept a drink from a friend who happens to be a girl."

For Septi, men and women are very different types of creatures. Men buy drinks for women, not the other way around. For the Dutch girl, men and women are roughly equal.

Meaning: For Septi, men and women are very different types of creatures. Men buy drinks for women, not the other way around. For the Dutch girl, men and women are roughly equal. This difference can be attributed to the dimension of masculinity/femininity. The Romanian is more masculine, which makes his relationship with a girl asymmetrical. This accounts for most of the girl's amazement. On top of that, Septi's actions speak of short-term orientation; immediate reciprocation of gifts, regardless of the cost, is important. The Dutch, on the other hand, find it reasonable to always keep the future of their wallets in the back of their heads. They are long-term oriented.

EXPLORING CULTURE

A Tale of Two Stairways

Mrs. Ngo, a woman from Cameroon, was studying at a Dutch university. A professor whom she was having an interview with showed her out of his office at the end of the interview. As she was heading toward the long way out of the building, he pointed out to her a staircase that provided a shortcut. "Oh," she exclaimed, "I thought that stairway was for staff only." This greatly amazed the Dutch professor, because stairways for staff only do not exist at Dutch universities, so he asked her what had made her think that the stairway was limited to staff use only. She replied that she had seen a staff member use it.

This incident describes a mild case of cultural misunderstanding. Can you identify which words and phrases point to this, then underline them? When you have done this, read on and find out how we have interpreted the incident.

Mrs. Ngo, a woman from Cameroon, was studying at a Dutch university. A professor whom she was having an interview with showed her out of his office at the end of the interview. As she was heading toward the long way out of the building, he pointed out to her a staircase that provided a shortcut. "Oh," she exclaimed, "I thought that stairway was **for staff only**." This greatly **amazed** the Dutch professor, because stairways **for staff only do not exist at Dutch universities**, so he asked her what had made her think that the stairway was limited to staff use only. She replied that she had **seen a staff member use it.**

Discussion: Identity and Hierarchy

Spot the concept: Identity and power distance are the core issues in this story.

Analysis: Mrs. Ngo comes from a collectivist country where rights and privileges vary by group, whereas the teacher comes from an individualist culture where everybody is supposed to have the same rights. Also, Mrs. Ngo comes from a culture of large power distance, and the university lies in a country of small power distance, the Netherlands. This combination of circumstances made her expect that she would have to use another staircase than the one reserved for people of higher status. It is clear that Mrs. Ngo was observing the situation around her very carefully, paying attention to symbols of role or status or group membership that would help her know what to expect of others and what others were expecting of her. She was anxious to behave appropriately in this new and unfamiliar setting.

Meaning: Mrs. Ngo was applying her own back-home rules for interpretation to the unfamiliar setting of the Dutch university. For the moment, her back-home rules are the only rules she has, until she learns the new rules. As she gathers information about the Dutch university context, she will no doubt begin to experience change in her perception, interpretation, and attribution. Mutual questioning and clarification of the kind that occurred between her and the professor will be beneficial to this process.

A Small Country?

At an international conference in Helsinki, the capital of Finland, Jorma Ollila, the president of Nokia Corporation, was addressing a large audience. After his speech one of the delegates stood up, announced himself loudly to be X from country Y, and asked without further introduction, "How can it be that such a small country as Finland can produce such a large, successful company?" Ollila smiled and replied, "That is an interesting question. I am open for suggestions."

Please underline those words and phrases that point to cultural differences. When you have done this, read on and find out how we have interpreted the incident.

At an international conference in Helsinki, the capital of Finland, Jorma Ollila, the president of Nokia Corporation, was addressing a large audience. After his speech one of the delegates stood up, **announced himself loudly** to be X from country Y, and asked **without further introduction**, "How can it be that such a **small country** as Finland can produce such a **large, successful company?**" Ollila **smiled** and replied, "That is an interesting question. **I am open for suggestions.**"

Discussion: Gender

Spot the concept: Large and *small* are the key words here. The aspect of culture that is involved is the degree of masculinity versus femininity.

Analysis: Mr. X seemed to believe that the size of a country is one of the causal factors that influence the size and success of its companies. His direct way of putting this might easily have been taken by Ollila as an attack on Finland. After all, Finland is not so small. However, Ollila chose to respond not by counterattacking but by playing down the attack. He probably did not take the question at all seriously, but did not want to reveal his feelings. Nor did he want to say something that boiled down to "Nokia is so successful because of me," probably because he did not want to brag.

Meaning: Mr. X acted in an aggressive way, consistent with a masculine culture. The view he expressed was in line with "Big is beautiful." Actually, there is no empirical basis for the opinion that big countries produce more successful companies than do small ones. The response by Jorma Ollila reflects femininity. In a feminine culture, fighting or aggressive behavior is not acceptable, and powerful people try to appear less powerful than they are. Ollila did not counter the attack but smiled it away, and he did not say how good he was but left that to the audience to infer. Incidentally, this incident illustrates the fact that cultural femininity is by no means a liability for business achievement.

By now, you might have an idea as to the whereabouts of country Y....

In a feminine culture, fighting or aggressive behavior is not acceptable, and powerful people try to appear less powerful than they are.

How Would You Feel? (Revisited)

Having practiced your ability to spot cultural differences, you are in a position to revisit the anecdotes from chapter 1. You can now better determine what orientations on the five dimensions may have guided your preferences.

First, look back to chapter 1, pages 12–14, to see what options you chose, then read in this section the explanations of cultural values that may have informed your choice. If you hesitated between options in chapter 1, it may have been because of your combination of values. After all, you are not one dimensional culturally, whereas the options were chosen to evidence one dimension of culture. Note that the responses that you did not choose, some of which may have made you feel quite indignant, could be wholly acceptable from a culturally different point of view. Also note that you may have had different reasons for choosing an answer than the one presented here. For instance, your personal history may have guided you to make a choice quite different from what your average fellow countryman or -woman might choose. And finally, your personality may have led you to give answers that are atypical for people from your country.

The Shabby Guitar Player

You are in a restaurant having dinner with an acquaintance. A shabby man with a guitar comes to your table and offers to play. How do you feel about this?

1. This man is a beggar and should find a job.

   This is a masculine point of view; the man is a loser. It could also speak of long-term orientation.

2. This man is filthy and disgusting.

   People from uncertainty avoiding cultures would feel this way. They might even be afraid of contracting a disease from the man.

3. This man is to be pitied.

   People from feminine societies might feel this way.

4. You do not know this man, and you have nothing to do with him.

   If you and your acquaintance are from a collectivist society and belong to a group to which the newcomer does not belong, then you might feel this way. But you might also feel this way if you are from an individualist, masculine culture. In that case you might not feel any moral obligation to care for a loser who caused his own misfortune and who is nothing to you.

5. Could be interesting. Maybe he plays well.

   This is how people from uncertainty tolerant cultures might feel. A novel, ambiguous situation piques their curiosity.

6. The waiter should remove this man.

   People from cultures high on power distance might feel this way. Or it might indicate strong uncertainty avoidance: the man is out of place in a restaurant and that is unsettling.

A Meeting in the Street

You are walking along the street in a town that is not your own. The street is quiet. Somebody crosses the street and walks toward you. What do you think?

1. This person means to rob you.

   People from a masculine culture might feel this way. In a masculine culture, strangers don't trust each other. If this culture is also strongly uncertainty avoiding, this would add to the distrust.

2. This person means to ask for directions.

   In feminine countries, people tend to trust strangers, and they might feel this way.

3. This person means to have a chat with you.

   This is an uncertainty tolerant point of view. It might also speak of collectivism: taking time for socializing.

4. This person might invite you to dinner.

   A person from a collectivist culture might have this expectation if the person has reason to expect that he or she will be considered part of the ingroup.

5. This person is going to tell you that you are not allowed to be here.

   Somebody from an uncertainty avoiding country might think this, particularly if power distance is also large.

6. This person means to sell you something.

   This might occur in many countries, but it is more likely to happen in collectivist nations, where personal contact and trade are more mixed than in individualist ones.

A Welcome at the Airport

You are headed to a formal business meeting with somebody you have never met before. When you get off the airplane, a warmly smiling woman wearing jeans and sandals is holding up a sign with your name on it. What do you think?

1. She must be a secretary.

   In a masculine society, gender roles are unequally distributed, and people might have this expectation.

2. She is probably the person with whom you will have the meeting.

   This expectation could indicate both femininity (you are not amazed that your important partner is a woman) and uncertainty tolerance (you are not taken aback because she is casually dressed).

3. It is wonderful to be welcomed so warmly.

   This is how somebody from a collectivist society might feel—or indeed anybody who does not take offense.

4. How dare someone meet you in such an informal outfit.

   This might be the reaction of an important person from a large power distance culture, who would have expected an impressive delegation.

5. There must be an error, because you were expecting a formal-looking gentleman.

   This would be a typical uncertainty avoiding reaction. If uncertainty avoidance is strong, people are expected to display their position through their clothing, and this woman is not dressed at all formally.

The Intruder

You are standing at a reception, engaged in conversation with another person you vaguely know. Suddenly a third person arrives and starts to talk to your conversation partner without seeming to notice you. What do you think?

1. This must be a close friend of your conversation partner.

   This would be the expectation of a person from a collectivist culture.

2. This must be an absolute brute to push you aside in this manner.

   Somebody from a feminine culture might feel this way.

3. Your conversation partner should ask the intruder to wait a moment.

   The reaction indicates individualism: you speak with one person at a time. This way of dealing with time is known as monochronic.

4. This must be a VIP (Very Important Person).

   This thought indicates large power distance.

5. This must be somebody with a very urgent matter.

   Somebody from an individualist culture might think this way; tasks prevail over relationships.

6. Your conversation partner should introduce you to the newcomer.

   This would be a collectivist expectation. Your conversation partner can include you in his or her ingroup to which the intruder apparently belongs. In almost all societies, this option would be more acceptable than the next one.

7. Nothing.

   This might be the reaction of somebody from an individualist, masculine culture; this is normal, acceptable behavior.

What Would You Do? (Revisited)

This section works in exactly the same way as the previous one does, except that you will refer back to pages 15–16 to see what options you chose.

The Returning Athlete

You are the mayor of a small town. An athlete from your town took part in the Olympic Games. The athlete is due to return tomorrow, having obtained fourth place in an event. What sort of official welcome will you prepare for her?

1. None, because a fourth place is not worth anything. If only it had been a gold medal....

   This is a masculine reaction. Only winning counts.

2. None, because there is no protocol for officially receiving returning sports players or participants.

   This reaction speaks of uncertainty avoidance: rules are rules.

3. A grand one, because even if she did not win, she did participate in the Olympic Games and that is a great achievement.

   This reaction speaks of a feminine perspective along with short-term orientation. It is feminine because participating is more important than winning. It is short-term oriented because if you are happy, you want to show it!

4. A grand one, because she is one of us and she has honored our town.

   This is a collectivist perspective, along with short-term orientation. When a member of the family comes home, you celebrate.

5. You will ask the city council for advice.

   This reaction indicates small power distance—not deciding alone but consulting others is considered appropriate.

The Accident

You are chairing a very important business meeting, for which some attendees have made a transoceanic flight. Millions of dollars are involved. During the meeting one of your local colleagues, a financial expert, receives a message: his eight-year-old child has been hit by a car and is hospitalized with very severe injuries. How do you react?

1. You cancel the meeting and arrange for a sequel on the following day.

   This is a feminine response. It symbolizes that you let personal matters prevail over business matters. The response may also indicate collectivism; you cancel the meeting because as "head of the family," you have to help your colleague first.

2. You let your colleague leave the meeting.

   This is an individualist response. The news only concerns that particular colleague, and you let that person deal with it.

3. You leave the room for a moment with your colleague and tell him that although you would like him to stay, he can leave if he wants to.

   This reaction speaks of small power distance. You do not decide on your own, but let the person have a say.

4. You go on with the meeting, asking your colleague to stay.

   This is a masculine reaction; the task comes first. It could also indicate uncertainty avoidance; time is money and flexibility is not popular. And it could indicate individualism; the colleague is no more important to you than the foreign visitors are.

Train or Car?

You are a commuter. The car trip to work takes approximately one hour, the train ride, approximately an hour and a half. Do you prefer to go by car or by train?

1. By car, because if I travel by train, people will think I can't afford a car.

   A masculine perspective. It also indicates short-term orientation: showing off.

2. By car, because it is faster.

   This is a typical masculine perspective. Being fast is a virtue in itself.

3. By car, because it is private.

   The car offers individual freedom, not loneliness. An individualist perspective.

4. By car, because people in my position do not travel by public transport.

   This could be the preference of an important person from a culture where power distances are large and uncertainty avoidance is strong.

5. By train, because it is safer.

   People from a feminine, individualist, long-term oriented society might reason thus; caring for their personal safety is considered important.

6. By train, because it allows me to get some work done while traveling.

   In this reaction, there is masculinity (get work done) and long-term orientation (saving time) and possibly uncertainty tolerance (you never know where you will sit in the train, but you still expect to be able to work).

7. By train, because I might meet interesting people.

   This is a typical uncertainty tolerant, short-term oriented attitude.

8. By train, because it is better for the environment.
   People from a feminine society would reason thus. It also indicates long-term orientation; the traveler forgoes the immediate advantage of faster travel for the future benefit of cleaner air.

9. Either way is fine, whichever is cheaper in the long run.
   This thrifty attitude is typical of long-term orientation.

A Virtual Contact

On the Web you have found the site of somebody you might want to start a business relationship with. How would you establish the first contact?

1. Write a formal, polite paper letter on your company's letterhead.

   This speaks of uncertainty avoidance. It must be noted, though, that e-mails are gradually becoming more accepted, even in countries of strong uncertainty avoidance.

2. Send an e-mail starting "Dear Mr. so-and-so" and ending "Kind regards, X."

   This is a feminine style, emphasizing a friendly relationship between the addressee and yourself.

3. Send an e-mail starting "My name is X and I have a proposal that might interest you" and ending with your first name.

   This is an individualist, masculine style. You briefly introduce yourself as an individual and then get down to business.

4. Have your secretary arrange a phone call.

   This approach indicates large power distance. It will convey your status to the person.

5. Call the person on the phone yourself.

   This seems to indicate femininity, because it can lead to a personal contact. It certainly indicates uncertainty tolerance, since you establish a two-way contact with very little idea how the conversation will proceed.

Attribution Exercises

In the stories above you were asked to give cultural explanations only. This is not always appropriate, as you have probably noticed when you tried to account for your own preferences. Your own experiences as well as your personality have contributed to your choice of alternatives.

You will now extend the scope of explanations to include personal attributes such as character or personal history. Read the following dialogues. Try to account for B's response, giving either cultural or personal preferences. Then read the suggested reasons and see whether your account fits in.

Long Time No See

A and B meet on the street. They have not seen one another for months.

> A: Hi, my friend!
>
> B: Oh, hello.
>
> A: How are you? Long time no see! Hey, let's go have a drink!
>
> B: I'm fine. You okay? Listen, I'm sorry, I've got to run. I'll give you a call soon, promise (goes away)!

What is the matter with B? Why might he not want to go have a drink? What are B's intentions? Choose one or more options.

1. B is in a hurry because of other tasks.

2. B does not really like A very much but does not wish to tell him so.

3. B is a conscientious worker and has to get back to work.

4. B wants to avoid hurting A's feelings but does not really intend to call him up.

5. B really means to give A a call soon.

6. B knows that A is very talkative and B does not have much time. B would rather call another time for a real meeting than have a brief half-baked chat now.

7. B is just shy.

Here are the perspectives that make the various responses meaningful.

1. B is in a hurry because of other tasks.

   This is a possible reason if B is from an individualistic and not very feminine culture. Time is carefully scheduled, and letting tasks prevail is acceptable.

2. B does not really like A very much but does not wish to tell him so.

   This is a possible reason if B is from a collectivistic culture.

If A is from a collectivistic culture, he or she may well feel rebuffed by B after this exchange.

3. B is a very conscientious worker and has to get back to work.
   This is a character attribute. If A is from a long-term oriented culture, he is likely to accept B's behavior as showing dedication to his work.

4. B wants to avoid hurting A's feelings but does not really intend to call him up.
   This could be the case if B is from a collectivistic and/or short-term oriented culture. If A is from such a culture, he may not expect B to call.

5. B really means to give A a call soon.
   This can be the case if B is from a long-term oriented culture, and A would expect it if he is from such a culture.

6. B knows that A is very talkative and B does not have much time. B would rather call another time for a real meeting than have a brief half-baked chat now.
   This is a matter of personal history between A and B.

7. B is just shy.
   This is a personal attribute, possibly having to do with B's relationship with A.

8. You may have had your own personal reasons for choosing another option. Incidentally, if you often choose your own option in this kind of exercise, that might indicate that you are from an individualist culture (you are supposed to have your own opinion) and possibly from a masculine one (you are not prepared to choose one of the available options for the sake of adapting yourself) or an uncertainty avoiding one (if you feel the options that the authors give are not specific enough).

None of Your Business

B is walking across a lawn in a park when A intervenes. They do not know one another.

> A: Hey! You! Get off that lawn!
>
> B: This is none of your business (does not budge).

Why does B not obey A?

1. B is a fearless person.

2. B has no respect for figures of authority.

3. B is a high-status person and believes A to be of inferior status.

4. B happens to be the owner of the lawn.

5. B happens to be a friend of the owner of the lawn.

Here are the perspectives that make the various responses meaningful.

1. B is a fearless person.

   This is a character attribute.

2. B has no respect for figures of authority.

   This can be the case if B is from a culture of small power distance.

3. B is a high-status person and believes A to be of inferior status.

   This can be the case if B is from a culture of large power distance.

4. B happens to be the owner of the lawn.

   This is a matter of personal history.

5. B happens to be a friend of the owner of the lawn.

   This is a matter of personal history and points to a collectivist cultural background on B's part.

Debriefing

In these dialogues, did you explain B's behavior by making assumptions about his or her personal history, character, or cultural background? On the basis of these dialogues, there is no way to decide which type of explanation is most valid! If you were A, how could you get to know the reason for B's behavior? You would need to acknowledge the possible types of reasons for the response, and then you could ask B, however hard that might be! Conversely, B could have helped A by explicitly formulating the intention behind his or her behavior. In the first dialogue, for example, B might have given a reason for running off that was acceptable to A. In the second dialogue, B might have explained to A why he or she did not leave.

Conclusion

You have now seen that culture is a complex phenomenon. In our world with its myriad cross-national activities, national culture is obviously an important variable, even though we have not been able to say the last word about it. People working with culturally different colleagues or clients and struggling with practical problems in multicultural settings understand the urgency for more accurate and appropriate guidelines for cross-cultural training. Culture is complex, but it is not chaotic; there are clearly defined patterns to be discovered.

In the fairy tale the family could not agree on what was the best culture. Of course, this is a universal truth: there simply is no best culture. Most people within a culture feel that their culture is better than others and try to tell others, "Look how good our culture is! Why don't you do like us?" But this is naive, particularly for today's world. We must learn to accept that cultures are different and to cooperate all the same. This is inherently very hard to do, because we perceive the values of our culture in moral terms, and therefore we tend to view other people's values as morally inferior. Our difficult task is to realize, while remaining proud of the good things in our own culture, that ours is just one culture, with no claim to moral superiority.

Culture is complex, but it is not chaotic; there are clearly defined patterns to be discovered.

We perceive the values of our culture in moral terms, and therefore we tend to view other people's values as morally inferior.

You are now familiar with the five dimensions of national culture that correspond to the five big issues in social life: identity, hierarchy, gender, truth, and virtue. It is now time to isolate each dimension into two role profiles that literally take the dimensions to their extremes. These are the ten synthetic cultures. In Part II you will learn about the ten synthetic cultures and gain practice identifying and using them in exercises. These activities with synthetic cultures bring cultural communication patterns to life.

Part II
Synthetic Cultures

Chapter 3

The Ten Synthetic Culture Profiles

This chapter presents the ten synthetic culture profiles in a format suitable for use during activities and simulations. Synthetic cultures embody the big issues of national cultures. The ten synthetic cultures are derived from Geert Hofstede's work on dimensions of national culture that you met in the fairy tale in chapter 2 and learned to recognize in exercises in that chapter. Each of the five big issues gives rise to two synthetic cultures. These are extreme manifestations of the value orientations at both ends of that dimension. Since the synthetic cultures represent single aspects only, and extreme forms at that, each of them is, so to speak, "obsessed" with one aspect of social life. Obviously, these synthetic cultures are simplifications; they do not exist in the real world, although the tendencies they demonstrate do exist. The dimensions with their attendant synthetic cultures are the following:

Synthetic cultures are extreme manifestations of the value orientations at both ends of each dimension.

- Identity (*Indiv* for extreme individualism, *Collec* for extreme collectivism)
- Hierarchy (*Hipow* for extremely large power distance, *Lopow* for extremely small power distance)
- Gender (*Mascu* for extreme masculinity, *Femi* for extreme femininity)
- Truth (*Uncavo* for extremely strong uncertainty avoidance, *Unctol* for extreme uncertainty tolerance)

- Virtue (*Lotor* for extreme long-term orientation, *Shotor* for extreme short-term orientation).

The table below shows how pairs of synthetic cultures are at the opposite end of one dimension of culture.

The Five Dimensions of Culture and Ten Synthetic Cultures

Dimension	One Extreme	Other Extreme
Identity	Indiv	Collec
Hierarchy	Hipow	Lopow
Gender	Mascu	Femi
Truth	Uncavo	Unctol
Virtue	Lotor	Shotor

The countries to which the five sisters in the fairy tale had immigrated exemplify five of the ten synthetic cultures. Satu's daughter lived in an Indiv country, Dua's son lived in a Lopow country, Tiga's daughter was from a Femi country, Ampat's son, an Uncavo country, and Lima's daughter, a Lotor country.

How to Interpret the Profiles

Each of the ten profiles consists of the following components:

- *Core value.* This is a rephrasing of the dimension extremity of this particular synthetic culture. It represents the *"obsession"* of this synthetic culture.

- *Core distinction.* This represents the *most central distinction* that members of the synthetic culture make when observing the social world around them.

- *Seven key elements.* These are *seven golden rules* for appropriate behavior in this culture. They describe aspects of home or working life.

- *Words with a positive connotation.* These are words that members of the synthetic culture *like to use and like to hear.* Used in arguments, these words enhance acceptability of one's position.

- *Words with a negative connotation.* These are words that members of the synthetic culture *do not like to use or to hear*. People who want to win arguments don't use these words.
- *At a glance.* The five headings of this section are the five cross-cultural communication barriers from chapter 1:
    1. Language. In theory there are usually no language barriers among members of each synthetic culture. Still, words may carry different connotations, and the context in which they are used may vary.
    2. Nonverbal behavior.
    3. Stereotypes imposed by outsiders.
    4. How outsiders tend to evaluate this synthetic culture.
    5. How the members of this synthetic culture behave under stress.
- *Gender roles.* Mascu and Femi, the synthetic cultures of the gender dimension, are the only ones with obviously different gender roles.

The synthetic culture approach described in this chapter provides a framework for organizing our experiences in a complex and dynamic world. The synthetic cultures are magnified versions of aspects of our value systems. As you read about them, you will recognize parts of yourself as well as parts of your family and friends.

Use your imagination while reading the profiles. For each of them, try to picture yourself as somebody who is proud of the values of that culture. Try to react with joy when you read the positive words and with disgust when you read the words with a negative connotation. Then you will acquire the "gut feeling" of that synthetic culture. You will also come to realize which of the synthetic cultures are close to your own values and which are not.

The synthetic cultures are magnified versions of aspects of our value systems.

Extreme Individualism (Indiv)

Core value
  individual freedom

Core distinction
  me/others

The Indiv culture is highly individualist.

Profiles: Identity Dimension

Seven key elements:

1. Honest people speak their mind.
2. Low-context communication (explicit concepts) is preferred
3. The task takes precedence over relationships.
4. Laws and rights are the same for all.
5. Trespassing leads to guilt and loss of self-respect.
6. Everyone is supposed to have a personal opinion on any topic.
7. The relationship between employer and employee or between parent and child is a contract based on mutual advantage.

Words with a positive connotation: self, friendship, "do your own thing," contract, litigation, self-interest, self-respect, self-actualizing, individual, dignity, I, me, pleasure, adventure, guilt, privacy.

Words with a negative connotation: harmony, face, obligation, sacrifice, family (in a symbolic sense), tradition, decency, honor, duty, loyalty, shame.

Indivs at a glance:

- Language: Indivs are verbal and self-centered, using *I* and *me* a lot.

- Nonverbal: Indivs make eye contact freely. When in groups, they are likely to stand out visually.

- Stereotypes: Indivs are defensive and tend to be loners; they run from one appointment to the next.

- Evaluation: Indivs use other people and measure the importance of others in terms of how useful they are.

- Stress: Indivs are supposed to continually test their own ability. This can be stressful. They tend to take on stress physically.

Gender roles: Females might as easily hold power as males, especially in urban and modernized areas. Gender roles are not rigidly defined; each gender takes on the role of the other when necessary to serve her or his self-interests in public and/or private activities.

Role of women: Women are supposed to be adventurous.
Role of men: Men are supposed to be adventurous.

Extreme Collectivism (Collec)

Core value
group harmony

Core distinction
ingroup/outgroup

The Collec culture is the opposite of the Indiv culture. It is extremely collectivist.

Seven key elements:

1. Members of one's ingroup (organization, extended family) are very close, whereas other, outgroup people are very distant.

2. Harmony should always be maintained and direct confrontations avoided.

3. Relationships are more important than the task at hand. Much time is spent on greeting and farewell rituals.

4. Laws, rights, and opinions differ by group.

5. Trespassing leads to shame and loss of face for the entire ingroup.

6. The relationship between employer and employee is perceived in moral terms, like a family link.

7. Spoken communication uses imprecise style. Discreet nonverbal clues, such as tone and pauses, are crucial. The speaker adapts to the listener.

Words with a positive connotation: we, harmony, face, obligation, sacrifice, family (in a symbolic sense), tradition, decency, honor, duty, loyalty, shame.

Words with a negative connotation: self, friendship, "do your own thing," contract, litigation, self-interest, self-respect, self-actualizing, individual, dignity, I, me, pleasure, adventure, guilt, privacy.

Collecs at a glance:

- Language:
  Collecs can be very silent, especially when alone among outgroup people. They use *we* instead of *I*. Silences may occur in conversations without creating tension.

- Nonverbal:
  Collecs are physically very close with ingroups, but reserved with outgroups.

- Stereotypes: They are never on their own; they are not forthright.
- Evaluation: Collecs will go to great lengths for their friends and expect the same in return.
- Stress: Collecs internalize stress. They will suffer if they cannot avoid deviant behavior or if they are forced to be alone. If provoked, they can be collectively violent to outgroups.

Gender roles: Gender roles are likely to be well defined, with males and females weaving the social fabric, each in his or her own sphere. Couples are part of wider family groups.

Role of women: Collec women tend to move into their partner's family when they marry. They tend to both care for the home and provide food and income.

Role of men: Men tend to spend much of their time in the social sphere of their work.

Extremely High Power Distance (Hipow)

Core value
respect for status

Core distinction
powerful/dependent

The Hipow culture is characterized by large power distance.

Profiles: Hierarchy Dimension

Seven key elements:
1. Might makes right; power is good.
2. Power, status, and privilege go together.
3. Less powerful people are dependent on those who are more powerful.
4. Centralization is popular.
5. Subordinates and children expect direction. They do not speak without being asked.
6. The ideal boss is a benevolent autocrat or "good father."
7. Style of speech is formal and acknowledges hierarchical positions.

Words with a positive connotation: respect, father (as a title), master, servant, older brother, younger brother, wisdom, favor, protect, obey, orders, pleasing.

Words with a negative connotation: rights, complain, negotiate, fairness, necessity, codetermination, objectives, question, criticize.

Hipows at a glance:

• Language:	Hipows are very verbal but usually soft-spoken and polite.
• Nonverbal:	Hipows are usually restrained and formal.
• Stereotypes:	Hipows are hierarchical and seek to please in a formal way.
• Evaluation:	Hipows tend to shift blame downward for any problems.
• Stress:	Hipows internalize stress and express it indirectly.

Gender roles: Both males and females may hold leadership roles. Either way it is obvious who holds power.

Role of women: In home and family affairs, women are

likely to be very powerful even though that power might be less visible than that of the males. While women may seem subservient, that may not in fact be true.

Role of men: While males may be the visible traditional leaders, the men may be much more subservient in less visible and more private social roles in a balance of power.

Extremely Low Power Distance (Lopow)

Core value
equality between people

Core distinction
responsible for task X/ not responsible for task X

The Lopow culture is the opposite of the Hipow culture. It is characterized by extremely small power distance.

Seven key elements:

1. Inequalities among people should be minimized. Privileges and status symbols are frowned upon.
2. There should be, and is, interdependence between less and more powerful people.
3. Hierarchy in organizations means an inequality of roles only, established for convenience.
4. Decentralization is popular.
5. Subordinates and children expect to be consulted.
6. In a conversation anyone can take the lead at any time.
7. Powerful people try to appear less powerful than they are.

Words with a positive connotation: rights, complain, negotiate, fairness, task, necessity, codetermination, objectives, question, criticize.

Words with a negative connotation: father (as a title), master, servant, older brother, younger brother, wisdom, favor, protect, obey, orders, pleasing.

Lopows at a glance:

- Language: Lopows talk freely in any social context.
- Nonverbal: Lopows are usually informal and unceremonious.
- Stereotypes: Lopows are unruly, impolite, and jealous.
- Evaluation: Lopows will talk back to anybody.
- Stress: Lopows always talk or fight conflicts out.

Gender roles: Leadership roles may be held by either male or female. It is not obvious to outsiders who holds leadership roles. Leaders have limited power and have to be resourceful democrats; otherwise, they would be ousted.

Role of women: Women may play any social role.
Role of men: Men may play any social role.

Extreme Masculinity (Mascu)

Core value
winning

Core distinction
man/woman

The Mascu culture is strongly masculine.*

Profiles: Gender Dimension

Seven key elements:

1. Material success and progress are dominant values.

2. Bigger and faster are better.

3. Men are supposed to be assertive, ambitious, and tough. Women should be subservient and tender. Attractive women can use their beauty as a weapon in social competition.

4. Mascus like to admire exceptional achievements or people.

5. Failing (at school, at work, in sports, or wherever) is a disaster.

6. Conflicts are resolved by arguing or fighting them out.

7. The best student, worker, or manager sets the norm.

Words with a positive connotation: career, competition, fight, aggressive, assertive, success, winner, deserve, merit, excel, force, big, fast, tough, quantity, total, power, action.

Words with a negative connotation: caring, solidarity, modesty, compromise, help, love, grow, small, soft, slow, tender, touch.

Mascus at a glance:

- Language: Mascus are loud and verbal, with a tendency to criticize and argue with others.

- Nonverbal: Mascus like physical contact, direct eye contact, and animated gestures.

- Stereotypes: Mascus are macho, are hero- and status-oriented, and like winners.

---

* Power is central to both Mascu and Hipow culture, but in Mascu culture, it means *power to*—to force others to do what you want them to do. In Hipow culture, it means *power as an intrinsic characteristic* of a person, unrelated to any circumstance. Other people who perceive that power will respond, without needing coercion.

- Evaluation: Mascus are hard to please, tend to be overachievers, are defensive, and blame others for their mistakes.

- Stress: Mascus generate stress through fast-paced lifestyles.

Gender roles: This synthetic culture is all about differences between socially "masculine" and socially "feminine" behaviors. Men are typically more powerful and are highly favored in leadership roles. Women can act like "one of the guys," but they have to be extra tough to succeed. Passive and facilitating behaviors are tolerated for women but not for men. Men are stereotyped as strong and women as weak. Sexual achievement is important, too. Everybody tries to look young and vigorous.

> *Role of women:* Women tend to be either masculine in their personal style or subservient and docile (at least outwardly). Young and attractive women can use their beauty to win but have no romantic illusions. Older and less attractive women are at a great disadvantage.

> *Role of men:* Men are supposed to excel in areas requiring physical strength. Young, strong, tall, and attractive men are idealized as heroes and are admired or envied by others. Men see life as a game played by men, with women as cheerleaders.

Extreme Femininity (Femi)

Core value
  caring for others,
  especially the weak

Core distinction
  caring/needing care

The Femi culture is strongly feminine. It is the opposite of the Mascu culture.

Seven key elements:

1. Dominant values in society are caring for the weak and preservation (for example, of the environment).

2. Small and slow are beautiful.

3. Everybody is supposed to be modest, soft-spoken, and empathetic—men and women alike.

4. Femis play down exceptional achievements and people.

5. Conflicts are resolved through compromise and negotiation.

6. Equality, solidarity, and quality of work life are emphasized.

7. Society is permissive.

Words with a positive connotation: quality, caring, solidarity, modesty, compromise, help, love, grow, small, soft, slow, tender, touch.

Words with a negative connotation: career, competition, fight, aggressive, assertive, success, winner, deserve, merit, excel, force, big, hard, fast, tough, quantity, total, power, action.

Femis at a glance:

- Language: Femis do not raise their voices. They like small talk and agreement.

- Nonverbal: They don't take much room and are warm and friendly in conversation.

- Stereotypes: You cannot tell the men from the women. Losers are pampered. Femis complain about small things.

- Evaluation: Femis tend to pity others and themselves and to avoid excessive achievements.

- Stress: Femis have a hard time standing up for their rights or ending relationships.

Gender roles: Gender is not supposed to play a role among Femis. Men and women are considered socially equal. Homosexuality is not a threat. Love and tenderness are for men and women alike. Intimate relationships without sex are allowed. Children need love, and parents spend much time on them.

Role of women: Because women give birth and breastfeed, they tend to have breaks in their working lives when they have children. Otherwise they are equal to men.

Role of men: Men can fulfill any role that women can, in much the same way, without raising curiosity. They tend to work shorter hours when they have young children.

Extreme Uncertainty Avoidance (Uncavo)

Core value
certainty

Core distinction
true/false

The Uncavo culture is one of strong uncertainty avoidance.

Profiles: Truth Dimension

Seven key elements:

1. What is different is dangerous.

2. Familiar risks are accepted, but ambiguous situations and unfamiliar risks are feared.

3. Rules are important, even if the rules will never work.

4. Rigid taboos exist about what is dirty, wrong, or indecent.

5. Time is money.

6. There is only one truth and we have it.

7. Experts and specialization are valued.

Words with a positive connotation: structure, duty, truth, law, order, certain, pure, clear, secure, safe, predictable, tight.

Words with a negative connotation: maybe, creative, conflict, tolerant, experiment, spontaneous, relativity, insight, unstructured, loose, flexible.

Uncavos at a glance:

- Language: Uncavos are very verbal and well organized, somewhat loud, and emotional.

- Nonverbal: Uncavos are animated in using hands but are uncomfortable with physical contact.

- Stereotypes: Uncavos have rigid beliefs and are obsessed with rules. They can be xenophobic. They argue all the time.

- Evaluation: Uncavos quickly and sometimes prematurely judge a situation to establish right and wrong.

- Stress: Uncavos are uptight. They externalize stress and usually make others feel stressed.

Gender roles: Appropriate male and female roles might or might not differ widely, but in any case, they are unambiguously defined and rigidly followed. Dress and behavior of men and women are defined by rules, traditions, and carefully guarded boundaries. Society has romantic and idealized images of gender roles.

Role of women: Women usually rule over home, family, children, and religious rituals. They may also be professionally active and tend to specialize in certain professions. Society can be very unforgiving of women who rebel or violate the rules, although elderly women may take on traditional power roles otherwise reserved for males.

Role of men: Professional qualifications are important for public identity. Men are expected to take care of women and to provide for the home and family. Older men are usually respected.

Extreme Uncertainty Tolerance (Unctol)

Core value
  exploration

Core distinction
  urgent/can wait

The Unctol culture is the opposite of the Uncavo culture. Even extreme ambiguity is tolerated well.

Seven key elements:

1. What is different causes curiosity.
2. Ambiguous situations and unfamiliar risks cause no discomfort.
3. Rules should be limited to those that are absolutely necessary.
4. Aggression and emotions should be hidden.
5. Being lazy feels good; working hard is valued only when needed.
6. Deviant and innovative ideas and behavior are tolerated.
7. Generalists are valued, as is common sense.

Words with a positive connotation: maybe, creative, conflict, tolerant, experiment, spontaneous, relativity, insight, unstructured, loose, flexible.

Words with a negative connotation: structure, duty, truth, law, order, certain, pure, clear, secure, safe, predictable, tight.

Unctols at a glance:

- Language: Unctols are not loud. They can be imprecise. They ask open-ended questions.

- Nonverbal: Unctols are unhurried, informal, and have no taboos.

- Stereotypes: Unctols have no principles and talk nonsense.

- Evaluation: Unctols judge in pragmatic, not moral, terms.

- Stress: Unctols are relaxed and take each day as it comes.

Gender roles: There may or may not be marked differences between men and women. People don't follow strict rules; exceptions are easily accepted. Personal relationships can take many forms. Homosexuality is not considered threatening.

Role of women: A wide range of roles is acceptable. A woman may easily adopt new roles if her situation in life changes.

Role of men: Men may or may not be expected to dominate over women. Deviant roles for men are acceptable.

Extreme Long-Term Orientation (Lotor)[†]

Lotor

Core value
  long-term benefits

Core distinction
  does/does not serve a purpose

The Lotor culture is extremely long-term oriented.

Profiles: Virtue Dimension

Seven key elements:
1. Working very hard is good.
2. Thrift and saving are good.
3. Never give up, even if results are disappointing.
4. People may devote their lives to lofty, remote ideals.
5. Traditions can be adapted to a modern context.
6. Achieving one's purpose may be worth losing face.
7. Past and future generations are important.

Words with a positive connotation: work, save, moderation, endurance, duty, goal, permanent, future, economy, virtue, invest, afford, effort.

Words with a negative connotation: relation, gift, today, yesterday, truth, quick, spend, receive, grand, tradition, show, image, the bottom line.

Lotors at a glance:

• Language:	Lotors are direct and focused, asking questions about implications of actions.
• Nonverbal:	Lotors are restrained and unceremonious.
• Stereotypes:	Lotors are dull and always working.
• Evaluation:	Lotors tend to blame themselves. They are careful planners.
• Stress:	Lotors can be uptight and worried. They can, however, cope with heavy workloads under difficult circumstances.

[†] For Western readers, here is a word of caution about the virtue dimension. This dimension was discovered using questionnaires designed by Asians. Western minds typically find the virtue aspect harder to grasp than they do the other aspects.

Gender roles: An elaborate system of social roles, ordered by status, exists in which men and women may have separate or overlapping spheres. If need be, they take on each other's role.

Role of women: Women work, whether or not they have children.

Role of men: Men tend to be entrepreneurial. The extended family may participate in business, and prosperity is desirable.

Extreme Short-Term Orientation (Shotor)

Core value
saving face

Core distinction
proper/improper

The Shotor culture is the inverse of the Lotor culture. It is very short-term oriented.

Seven key elements:

1. Never lose face.
2. There is a social pressure to "keep up with the Joneses," even if it means overspending.
3. Quick results are expected.
4. Traditions should be respected.
5. Social demands (for example, reciprocating gifts) are met regardless of cost.
6. Personal stability is much valued.
7. Saving is not popular, so that there is little money for investment.

Words with a positive connotation: relation, gift, today, yesterday, truth, quick, spend, receive, grand, tradition, show, image, the bottom line.

Words with a negative connotation: work, save, moderation, endurance, duty, goal, permanent, future, economy, invest, afford, effort.

Shotors at a glance:

- Language: Shotors talk a lot. They enjoy talking about the past.
- Nonverbal: Shotors are ceremonious, attentive, and stylish and are warm and formal.
- Stereotype: Shotors are big spenders, irresponsible.
- Evaluation: Shotors are fatalistic and live from day to day.
- Stress: Shotors are desperate to save face and are distressed at loss of face.

Gender roles: An elaborate system of social roles, ordered by status, exists. Much time is spent maintaining this system through traditional rituals in which men and women have definite roles. Women may or may not be subservient to men.

Role of women: Women know how to behave and are good hosts. They tend to give much attention to their looks.

Role of men: Men like to socialize and to womanize. They might fight for ideals, however impractical. They will respond to appeals for help in times of crisis but are poor at keeping long-term commitments. They will not do anything that might endanger their dignity.

Conclusion

You have now been introduced to the ten synthetic cultures. Here they appear once more in the summary table below. As you can see from the table, some of the synthetic cultures may seem to be similar in some social settings.

Summary of the Synthetic Cultures

Synthetic Culture	Obsessed with	Sound	Space	Time	Stereotypes
Indiv	individual freedom	loud	far	any	hurried, loners
Collec	group harmony	soft	close	any	never alone, devious
Hipow	respect for status	soft	far	any	seek to please
Lopow	equality between people	loud	close	any	unruly, jealous
Mascu	winning	loud	close	any	macho, competitive
Femi	caring for the weak	soft	close	any	sexless, complaining
Uncavo	certainty	loud	far	past	rigid, arguing
Unctol	exploration	soft	close	now, future	unprincipled, odd
Lotor	long-term virtue	soft	far	future	dull, workaholics
Shotor	face	soft	close	past, now	big spenders

In the next chapter you will start working with the synthetic cultures to see how they manifest themselves in social interaction.

Chapter 4

Getting to Know the Synthetic Cultures

In this chapter you will do a number of exercises to get acquainted with the synthetic cultures. You will follow the three-step approach that you are becoming familiar with. First, you will learn to be *aware* of synthetic cultural differences. Second, you will do exercises to increase your *knowledge* of the synthetic cultures. If you wish to practice your *skills* in playing synthetic culture profiles, you can use the materials in Part III of this book.

Here are two awareness exercises about cross-cultural encounters. Read the responses by fictitious persons from each synthetic culture, and try to understand why they react in the way they do. Note that in reality, people can have a similar reaction for various reasons, depending on their combination of values.

Cross-Cultural Encounters

You are at a reception. You notice a senior person who does not know you but whom you need to speak to. You walk up to that person and say, "Hi. How do you do. I am Toby." Here is how the other person, depending on which synthetic culture he or she was from, would feel.

- *Hipow.* The senior person would feel offended and might pretend not to notice you.
- *Lopow.* The person would not take offense and might start a conversation with you.
- *Indiv.* The person would not take offense and might give his or her own name in reply.
- *Collec.* The person would not be pleased but would show no emotion. He or she might politely ask you for your affiliation.
- *Mascu.* The person would check whether you could be of use. He or she might ask you what you want, or say "Hi" and walk away.
- *Femi.* The person would not take offense. He or she might briefly inform you about how he or she is doing and then inquire about your well-being.
- *Uncavo.* The person would be alarmed at being addressed so informally by an utter stranger. He or she might make excuses for not knowing you and try to escape or start to ask pointed questions to find out more about you.
- *Unctol.* The person would find it interesting to be addressed by a stranger. He or she might ask you an open-ended question, such as "and how do you like it here, Toby?"
- *Lotor.* The person would presume that you want something. He or she would be reserved and might try to find out what you want.
- *Shotor.* The person would not take offense. He or she would be warm and would probably chat for a while.

An Unexpected Meeting

You are about to board an airplane for an international flight. You are going home after visiting your sister who has emigrated. Police officers are searching all passengers for weapons, drugs, and so forth. To your surprise the officer who takes you to a cabin to be searched happens to be your sister's brother-in-law, whom you have met repeatedly. Here is how a person from each synthetic culture would react.

- *Hipow*. He would apologize for having to search you and then do so respectfully.
- *Lopow*. He would search you. He might make a joke such as "Next time you can search me," indicating his equality with you.
- *Indiv*. He would search you in a matter-of-fact way and then start a conversation.
- *Collec*. He would not search you, because you are family.
- *Mascu*. He would show off his search technique on you, and he might tell you about the terrible things he has found lately.
- *Femi*. He would search you gently.
- *Uncavo*. He would search you thoroughly.
- *Unctol*. He would not search you; instead you would have one more good chat together.
- *Lotor*. He would apologize, then search you.
- Shotor. He would not search you but tell you how happy he is to see you one more time.

This exercise shows that the same action can mean different things to different people depending on their cultural background.

Now it is time to increase your knowledge of the synthetic cultures. Here are some events that have happened during synthetic culture simulations. You can use them to test your understanding of the synthetic cultures. Answers are on page 119.

Guess the Synthetic Culture

1. A foreign consultant arrives at a meeting, coughing and sneezing. Instead of going to work, his hosts start to inquire after his health and to offer him tea and a warm coat. What is the synthetic culture of the hosts?

2. A single-culture meeting of a team is particularly noisy. Not only does everyone talk loudly, but also nobody listens to the others. They do not reach agreement during the meeting. What is their synthetic culture?

3. A consultant from an Anglo-style country visits a foreign team. The foreigners seem to be rather hesitant in their answers to his questions. They spend a little time looking at the table, and then one of them speaks up. The CEO is entirely silent and just sits there nodding his head. What is their synthetic culture?

4. A group of clients is being served in a cafe. When the waiter brings in fruit pies, they ask for a certificate, or some other form of formal proof of high hygienic quality of the pies. What is their synthetic culture?

5. In the same cafe, another group of clients asks for half the number of drinks for the number of people but with two straws in each glass. What is their synthetic culture?

6. At yet another table in this cafe, a waiter comes to take orders. When he asks the first person what she would like to drink, the customers start to talk among themselves and then the person addressed by the waiter replies, "We would like coffee and apple pie, please." What is their synthetic culture?

7. An important representative from a foreign country visits a Lopow team. He asks them for their opinions and expertise. They give them freely because they assume that he is being polite and will reciprocate. But when they have finished, he just says "Thank you" and leaves. What is his synthetic culture?

Answers

1. *Femi*. They see a person in need, not necessarily somebody they know, and their urge is to help. They are not aware that the consultant could be afraid of being considered a weakling. To them, needing help is not a disqualifier. On the contrary, it shows he is human.

2. *Indiv*. But that only accounts for the fact that everyone was voicing an opinion. All the participants were really from a masculine culture. That accounts for the lack of convergence: nobody was prepared to give in to the others.

3. *Hipow*. What the consultant has not perceived is that his hosts are in fact discreetly waiting for their CEO to nod his head toward one of them, indicating by that signal who is to reply to the question.

4. *Uncavo*. They are afraid of eating unclean food.

5. *Lotor*. This practice makes a little money go a long way.

6. *Collec*. They order as one person.

7. *Mascu*. This representative is using the team in an instrumental way—robbing them of their knowledge without giving anything in return, if you like.

Here are some hypothetical workplace situations to consider. Suppose that you are in a team of multinational managers who work together in a department of some organization. The question is how would most people in your team, which is made up of members from all of the synthetic cultures, respond to the following issues or behave in the following situations? Please supply answers appropriate for at least two synthetic cultures for each statement before reading on. (In the first workplace situation, possible answers are provided as an example of the procedure we are asking you to follow.) Answers begin on page 121.

Workthink

1. Around here, our attitude and behavior toward the president or CEO of the organization would be expressed like this:

   For example:
   Collec: He will provide for our families and for us.
   Uncavo: He offers stability and is technically competent.

2. If one of us made a technical mistake that cost the company a great deal of money, we would do the following:

3. If a technical mistake was publicly exposed by the media, we would say or do the following:

4. If one of us did not receive a promotion or special assignment that he or she believed was well deserved, that person would be likely to act in the following manner:

5. If one of us did get an unexpected promotion, he or she would be likely to do the following:

6. Our opinion about the role of methods in large projects (e.g., project management) is as follows:

7. If one of us was given a large incentive bonus because the team he or she leads exceeded its goal, he or she would do the following:

Possible Answers

What counts is not so much giving the "right" answers but the process of reflection involved in the choosing. Depending on the context that you assume, possible answers to these questions could vary a lot.

1. Around here, our attitude and behavior toward the president or CEO of the organization would be expressed like this:

    - Indiv: I work hard because she might recognize my achievements and help me get ahead.

    - Collec: He will provide for our families and for us.

    - Hipow: He is our father. We respect and obey him, and he looks after us.

    - Lopow: She should listen to us and be resourceful.

    - Mascu: He is our hero. He should be tough and decisive.

    - Femi: She is a person just like everybody else. She should care for the weaker among us.

    - Uncavo: He offers stability and is technically competent.

    - Unctol: She listens and has good judgment.

    - Lotor: He knows where the organization is heading.

    - Shotor: She is outgoing and knows how to meet deadlines.

Note: In all synthetic cultures but Mascu, *he* and *she* are interchangeable.

2. If one of us made a technical mistake that cost the company a great deal of money, we would do the following:

- Indiv: Fire her and hire someone else.
- Collec: Try to blame an outsider.
- Hipow: Try to relay the blame to the lowest echelon.
- Lopow: Hold that person responsible.
- Mascu: Conclude that this person is a loser and consider firing her.
- Femi: Feel sorry for the person and coach or educate him.
- Uncavo: Look down on this incompetent person.
- Unctol: Dismiss the problem; it is all in the game.
- Lotor: Realize that no punishment is necessary; that person's shame is punishment enough.
- Shotor: Dismiss the error with a warning as long as it does not show in the quarterly figures. If it does, however, fire the person and make a show of it.

3. If a technical mistake was publicly exposed by the media, we would say or do the following:

- Indiv: Identify a scapegoat and fire him.
- Collec: Feel very much ashamed and avoid admitting the mistake in public.
- Hipow: Curb the media in the future and denounce those who published the mistake.
- Lopow: Make the company's own viewpoint known to the media.
- Mascu: Feel very bad and might suffer ridicule or even dismissal, or counterattack the offending media.
- Femi: Find excuses for the mistake; after all, "Nobody's perfect."

- Uncavo: Be concerned about our reputation and attack the credentials of the offending media: "unschooled writer," "nonprofessional journalism."

- Unctol: View the situation as an opportunity for learning to do better the next time.

- Lotor: Launch a reeducation program to prevent repetition of the error.

- Shotor: Launch an immediate counteraction in the media to prove nothing was wrong.

4. If one of us did not receive a promotion or special assignment that he or she believed was well deserved, that person would be likely to act in the following manner:

- Indiv: Look for another, better job elsewhere.

- Collec: Swallow the blow and feel bad only if the job went to an outsider.

- Hipow: Swallow the disappointment; the boss will grant a promotion in due time.

- Lopow: Complain to the boss and request an explanation.

- Mascu: Feel beaten and wait for revenge.

- Femi: Try to downplay the incident; the other person, after all, may have been in greater need of the promotion.

- Uncavo: Ask for the specific reasons why the other candidate was judged better.

- Unctol: Accept it but begin to look for a better job elsewhere.

- Lotor: Revise his or her career plans.

- Shotor: Take some conspicuous action to restore face among colleagues.

5. If one of us did get an unexpected promotion, he or she would be likely to do the following:
    - Indiv: Buy new business cards to reflect her new title and tell people about "a new challenge" and "adventure."
    - Collec: Make sure his relatives benefit.
    - Hipow: Buy a bigger house or car to show increased status, because of possible anxiety about entering a new social sphere.
    - Lopow: Show everybody that she has remained the same.
    - Mascu: Buy a bigger car to boast about.
    - Femi: Make sure his family agree.
    - Uncavo: Feel anxious about the unknown; take formal training to prepare for the new responsibilities.
    - Unctol: Feel pleased and look forward to the new job.
    - Lotor: See it as the result of long, hard work and adapt her career planning.
    - Shotor: Throw a big party to celebrate and invite everybody.
6. Our opinion about the role of methods in large projects (e.g., project management) is as follows:
    - Indiv: Methods for empowerment and team building are important.
    - Collec: We manage by mutual adjustment. Methods are not very important.
    - Hipow: Methods are not really necessary. The boss decides anyhow.
    - Lopow: We need participatory methods.
    - Mascu: Only the top-notch methods that guarantee winning are of any use.

- Femi: We need methods that give the nonmanagerial workers a voice.

- Uncavo: Yes, they are very important for controlling time and budgets and must be meticulously adhered to.

- Unctol: Methods are for stupid people. Good, creative generalists are what we need.

- Lotor: Overall methods with the large view of the company's goals are preferred.

- Shotor: The bottom line should rise each quarter. That is what counts.

7. If one of us was given a large incentive bonus because the team he or she leads exceeded its goal, he or she would do the following:

- Indiv: Add the award to his resumé.

- Collec: Share the bonus with the team.

- Hipow: Make a formal speech to announce that her team had received this special distinction.

- Lopow: Be pleased and thank all the team members informally.

- Mascu: Try to get a big diploma documenting the bonus, frame it, and hang it prominently in his office.

- Femi: Share the bonus with those team members most in need of the money or give it to a good cause.

- Uncavo: Worry whether the bonus would result in new duties.

- Unctol: Be pleased and enjoy herself.

- Lotor: Put the money in a savings account.

- Shotor: Celebrate with the team and those who granted the bonus.

Synthetic Cultures versus Real Cultures

Working with synthetic cultures offers many training opportunities but does not address all aspects of culture. Here are some important points to bear in mind when working with synthetic cultures. To begin with, real cultures rarely fall in the extreme ends of any of the five continua, unlike the stereotyped synthetic cultures. Second, people perceive behaviors in relative terms. Consequently, cultural characteristics of foreigners, however extreme from the dimension model point of view, only become salient to them if those characteristics differ from their own. Then, very crucially, real cultures have elements of all dimensions—they are multidimensional. Finally, culture does not only vary across nations but also across regions, ethnic groups, and other boundaries.

We shall use a few true anecdotes to illustrate these four points.

Real Cultures, Not Extreme Cases

In each actual society, some elements of both extremes of each dimension can be found, depending on the situation.

In individualist societies everybody is responsible for his or her own behavior, and one usually doesn't feel ashamed of other people's behavior. This contrasts sharply with collectivist cultures, where the poor performance or bad behavior of one person can cast deep shame upon his or her family, company, or country. Yet in each actual society, some elements of both extremes of each dimension can be found, depending on the situation. For example, someone from an individualist culture can experience feelings of shame for his country, as the following account by a male Dutch student demonstrates.

EXPLORING CULTURE

Jokes in the Pub

The most striking experience I had took place in Antwerp, a Belgian town close to the Dutch border. With a few friends I went to the city to have a nice day. During the day we met a group of young Dutchmen and joined them. After having drunk some beers in the city, they started making insulting remarks to nearby Belgians and telling "jokes" at the Belgians' expense. Even when they ordered drinks in a bar, they were very rude and made insulting remarks to the barkeeper. I was very angry and actually ashamed of being seen as a Dutchman. Without arguing with the young men, our group told them that we wanted to go our own way, and that is what we did.

This example goes to show that in the real world, the two poles of a dimension of national culture (here, individualism and collectivism) are not as dissimilar as day and night. All people have to resolve issues of individual versus group identity, whether they were raised in an individualist culture or not. The Netherlands is a highly individualist country, but even so, the Dutch are not free from group identity. The storyteller felt ashamed of the behavior of his compatriots, not because he was responsible for it but because he was seen as belonging to their group. Yet the reaction of this Dutchman to his feelings of shame—his party left their countrymen without criticizing them—speaks of individualism.

Incidentally, we can also use this anecdote to argue that not every behavior can be explained by a reference to national culture. The insulting behavior by the other group of Dutch people can partly be explained by the fact that they are a group of adolescent males. All over the world, adolescent males have a tendency to gang up and bully other people, particularly when alcohol is involved.

Not every behavior can be explained by a reference to national culture.

Relativity of Behaviors

Two other cases make the point that each dimension of national culture is a continuum. Spain has a culture that is intermediate on the individualism–collectivism dimension; therefore a Spaniard sees some cultures as individualistic, others as collectivistic. Relative differences between cultures are what people perceive.

A young woman from Spain recounts the following story.

She Hates Being with Her Parents

This summer during my trip to England, my English friend, a girl my age, was guiding me through her town, York. That small and quiet town impressed me, so I asked her why she preferred to study in London and not in her native town, which looked to me ideal for studying and enjoying student life. Her reply shocked me. She argued that what keeps her far away from home is the fact that she hates being with her parents now. The only time she visits her family is Christmas. The word hate puzzled me so much that I just stood there gaping at her. She was aware of my reaction, because she told me I shouldn't be so surprised.

This account is by a male Spanish student.

Tickets or Packs?

In 1991 I went to Romania for one week in an exchange between student associations all over Europe. The economic situation of most of the population was desperate. We went on an excursion to the mountains for three days by train. We Spanish students bought our tickets, but the Romanians didn't. They said there was no need, that if the conductor came by to collect the tickets, a pack of cigarettes would be payment enough, and they were right. When we got to the hotel, instead of paying the prices that foreigners had to pay, we paid the prices for Romanians, which for us was nothing; we had only to give the man at the front desk a small tip in dollars. It wasn't much, but it was more than what we would have paid for the rooms. On the way back in the train, instead of the conductor, there were special railway inspectors who were supposed to be more severe. This time it took a small negotiation with them, and it cost two packs of cigarettes. But the funniest thing was that all the Romanians kept complaining about the government; everybody was talking about free-market economy, and they were all hoping to be like a Western country, but everybody's behavior in this country wasn't really going to improve the situation. They all wanted the state to keep paying for everything.

These two examples show that while Spanish culture is collectivist when compared with the English, it is individualist when compared with the Romanian one. In Spain family ties are much closer than in England. In Romania laws and rights differ by group much more than they do in Spain. Romanians and their friends were considered ingroup members compared with tourists, and only the latter needed train tickets and had to pay the full hotel fare. Northern Europeans often interpret Spanish behavior as corrupt, just as the Spanish student does for the Romanian behavior. Apparently, what people from more collectivistic cultures perceive as "caring for one's friends" is perceived as corruption or favoritism by those from more individualistic cultures.

What people from more collectivistic cultures perceive as "caring for one's friends" is perceived as corruption or favoritism by those from more individualistic cultures.

Multidimensionality of Real Cultures

When two cultures really feel strange to one another, it means that the two societies have resolved more than one of the big issues (identity, hierarchy, gender, truth, and virtue) differently. In terms of the five-dimension model, this is to say that the two differ on more than one dimension of culture. The following two anecdotes illustrate the case of the Netherlands and Japan.

During the early nineteen-nineties, Teikyo University of Japan started a junior college for 112 female Japanese students in Holland. These Japanese students stayed there for one year to visit Europe and learn some English. A group of Dutch students were paid to organize social activities for the Japanese girls. Here is the account of one of the Dutch students, a young man.

Maybe We Go Ice Skating

The Japanese girls never say yes right away when you propose something to them. For example, we wanted to go ice skating with the girls, but when we asked them to go, they said "Maybe." Then they talked with their friends. They asked many questions about what was going to happen, especially when it was something unknown to them. Many girls did not go ice skating because they had never done such a thing, and although we assured them that prior experience was not necessary, they were not convinced. When they finally did decide to go, they signed up as a group.

After an activity sometimes we asked for their opinion about that event. This was a very difficult question for them because they are not used to giving their own opinion. In general they would feel very shy and say things like "Difficult" and "I don't know." Sometimes, when the girls were in a small group, they started to talk in Japanese with each other and after a few minutes one would say, "We think that…." We have now substituted the opinion question for the question, "What have you seen?"

This account illustrates differences between the Dutch excursion leader and the Japanese girls on two dimensions: collectivism and uncertainty avoidance. The more collectivist Japanese are not used to the individualist Dutch habit of voicing their private opinion, and their strong uncertainty avoidance makes them nervous about engaging in unfamiliar activities. The two countries differ on yet another dimension of national culture, as the following episode demonstrates. It is told by the same excursion leader.

The Lost Set

Not long ago we played a volleyball tournament with the girls. We had three Japanese teams and about fifteen Japanese fans. All the other teams were Dutch. Our first Japanese team played very well due to good technique and a fanaticism that I had not seen with Dutch girls. When a girl made a mistake, she would blame herself heavily and apologize to her team members, the coach, and the public. The fans screamed and yelled at each point. Unfortunately, we lost one set, which was reason enough for the team to start crying. The fans and the other Japanese teams also started to cry because Teikyo had lost. We weren't sure how to comfort thirty Japanese girls and at the same time explain to the other teams that nothing serious had happened. After this outburst, though, we won the last game and therefore the competition, which earned us a nice trophy. The girls felt so happy that the party afterward lasted the whole night.

In this case a difference in masculinity between Japan and Holland is manifest. The Japanese are extremely high on the masculinity scale. This accounts for the fanaticism the Dutch leader had not seen with Dutch girls. It also means that gender roles in Japan are very wide apart. Nevertheless, both genders have the same attitude toward winning and losing. Losing a sports match is as devastating for females as it would have been for males. The Dutch, however, who are low on masculinity, do not make a big thing about losing a match. They felt that nothing serious had happened. Their concern reflects a feminine culture: to comfort the Japanese girls and to reassure the other Dutch teams that no harm had been done.

All in all we see that the two countries differ considerably on three of the five dimensions of culture.

National versus Cultural Boundaries

The stress on national cultural identity in this book should not leave you with the impression that all people in a country necessarily share the same culture. Any group of people can have cultural attributes of its own. In most countries regional, ethnic, or class differences cause separate groups with very different subcultures to form. This is obviously true for geographically large countries and between clearly distinguishable ethnic groups in a country. But even in a geographically small country such as the Netherlands, and even among populations that have lived close together for centuries, cultural differences may not follow national borders. Consider the following account by a young Dutchman.

In most countries regional, ethnic, or class differences cause separate groups with very different subcultures to form.

Dutch Stinginess

I was born in Kerkrade, a town in the south of the Netherlands very close to the German border. When I was a teenager, my family spent summer vacations mostly in Austria. Year after year I noticed that as a person from the South, a "Limburger," I felt quite different from a person from the North, a "Hollander."

In the hotels (Gasthöfe) where we stayed, our parents always let us choose from the menu what we wanted to eat. In Hollander families, on the contrary, the parents chose what they wanted to eat and asked for extra plates on which they put some of their own food for the children. At first I thought this odd behavior had to be a coincidence, but after experiencing it on many occasions, I decided to ask one of those Hollanders why he did not let his children order their own meal just like the parents. The father's reply was something like this: "They are lucky that we can afford this trip at all." To him we seemed to be rich, throwing away money by ordering so many meals.

I saw more instances of this difference. Whenever Hollanders ordered a wedge of pie, they split it between two people. Hollanders often ordered one glass with two straws for two people—and these were not couples in love with each other! A Limburger would have been ashamed to do such a thing: either you buy something for everybody or you buy nothing at all. The Germans have an expression for this: "Wenn schon, denn schon" ("If at all, then do it wholeheartedly"). In two Gasthöfe, the waitresses even came to our table and asked us if we were really from Holland and if so, why we were so different from the Hollanders. They felt we were friendlier, we ate more, and we were not as tight with our money as they were.

Since then, whenever a person in Austria asks me where I am from, I never call myself a Dutchman but always a Limburger from Kerkrade, near the border with Germany.

This story illustrates the fact that national and cultural boundaries do not always coincide. The Limburgers are more inclined to short-term orientation than the Hollanders are. The anecdote also shows how strongly culturally determined behaviors can be associated with feelings of pride and shame. It is very hard for this boy to say "Let the Hollanders be economical if they like" and not attach a moral judgment, and it is likewise difficult for the Hollander father not to condemn the Limburgers for throwing away their money.

Conclusion

You have now acquired a sense of how the synthetic cultures operate in social interaction. In the next chapter you will encounter full-fledged dialogues with members from the ten synthetic cultures.

Chapter 5

Dialogues in Synthetic Culture Role

This chapter* is specifically aimed at those who need to improve their skills in conducting cross-cultural interviews, but all readers can use the dialogues to get a feeling for how to act when they are having a conversation with someone from a different culture. Besides, there is no way to acquire cross-cultural skills without learning interviewing skills. Most decisions in the workplace are based on interview data. Interviewing is the most frequently used method for supervising or managing people. It may be done formally with a specific objective or informally while getting to know a person or situation. Interviewing may be directed toward employees, peers, superiors, customers, suppliers, clients, or the public. Typically the interviewer is a boss, colleague, human relations counselor, or a doctor. Interviewing is different from ordinary conversation in that it involves purposeful communication with another person. The purpose may be exchange of information, persuasion, employee counseling, problem solving, or decision making (e.g., selecting, orienting, training, developing, appraising, promoting, or terminating employees). While many people have

Interviewing is different from ordinary conversation in that it involves purposeful communication with another person.

* Portions of Pedersen and Ivey's *Culture-Centered Counseling and Interviewing Skills* (1993) were adapted for this chapter with permission from the publisher, Greenwood Press. That book provides numerous additional dialogues for Indiv, Hipow, Mascu, and Uncavo clients. It makes good reading for those who want to study various other skills that are important in counseling.

Cross-cultural settings add significantly to the complexity of the interview process and require special training.

a natural ability to interview, it is a skill that can be improved through training, even for the best interviewers.

Interviewing, consulting, and counseling deal with the human side of management, where the complexity of problems, personalities, and situations prohibits easy solutions or answers. Cross-cultural settings add significantly to the complexity of the interview process and require special training. Synthetic cultures have a successful track record for such training and for teaching cross-cultural communication skills in general.

The "interviewer" and "client" pair in the dialogues below can be any two people: host-visitor, boss-employee, doctor-patient, and so on. *The focus is not on the professional position of the pair but only on their feedback behavior in relation to the client's synthetic culture.* We have retained the general labels of "interviewer" and "client" for the sake of clarity.

Dialogues: Identity Dimension

Indiv (Individualism)

Indivs can do whatever they want, and their "freedom" and their "rights" are necessary values.

Indiv culture believes that people are supposed to take care of themselves and remain emotionally independent of groups, organizations, or other collectivities. Self-emphasis is important, even in building friendships. Indivs can do whatever they want, and their "freedom" and their "rights" are necessary values. They build contracts to protect their rights from others and to protect their dignity. Their high level of self-respect does not keep them from enjoying a good time and an occasional adventure, even if they might feel guilty later. When they are friendly, they are very verbal and open, but they can be very critical toward enemies. Indivs like to debate issues but will withdraw and become defensive with somebody they don't trust. When they are interested, they can be loud with lots of questions but they are likely to look away when they get bored. They judge another by how much they need the other.

Let us look at an interview with an Indiv client where the interviewer does not do a good job of giving culturally sensitive feedback.

Interviewer:	How are we feeling today (smiling and leaning back in the chair)?
Indiv:	I'm probably not feeling as good as you seem to be feeling (smiling sarcastically).
Interviewer:	(leaning forward over the desk and looking directly at the client) Are you embarrassed coming to see me? You seem angry.
Indiv:	I'm not angry...yet! And even if I am, that's my business.
Interviewer:	We aren't going to make much progress unless we work together.
Indiv:	(looking away) Why should I trust you? What's in it for me?
Interviewer:	You have an obligation to your family and to society; you also have a duty to make some sacrifices to help them like they have helped you.
Indiv:	Nobody ever helped me! And even if they tried, I wouldn't let them! I don't want to owe anybody. I'm my own person.
Interviewer:	You don't want help, do you! You just sit right there until you're ready to talk with me and let me help you.

The interviewer starts by prematurely presuming a unity between the interviewer and the client. The client responds defensively, and the interviewer gets defensive in return. The interviewer presumes a shared understanding of affiliate values, which the client rejects. This makes the interviewer still more defensive. The interviewer and client move steadily in opposite directions, with the interviewer advocating obligations and the client advocating independence. The interviewer also violates the guidelines for giving feedback by focusing on the person rather than the person's behavior to the point of almost attacking the client, by making negative inferences without adequate data, by giving unsolicited advice, and by becoming personally involved.

Let us look at a second interview between an interviewer and an Indiv client that has a more successful outcome.

Interviewer: I'm glad to see you came. I've been reading about your problem on the floor and looking forward to meeting you.

Indiv: It's a little hard coming here. I'm afraid the other guys will find out and think I can't solve my own problems. I'm afraid they'll lose respect for me.

Interviewer: Let's make a bargain. I'll do as much as I can if you'll do as much as you can. Is it a deal?

Indiv: Sure, it's a deal (they shake hands on it). Where shall I start? What should I tell you first? What can I do?

Interviewer: Good questions! You maybe already have some ideas about what works, so why don't you tell me what you think about the poor morale in your team and then I'll jump in when I have a question or something to add.

Indiv: Great! Maybe if you take one side and I take the other, we can find out what works!

The interviewer shows respect and interest in the client as a person, both by the way he or she addresses the client and by taking the trouble to do some homework before the interview. The client feels valued as an individual and willing to disclose some fears and facts to the interviewer that might not have been shared otherwise. The client is not threatened and instead forms an alliance with the interviewer. They will try to solve the problem together. The client sees the interviewer as potentially useful, as an ally, and sees working through his morale problem as an exciting challenge. The interviewer avoids making value judgments and focuses just on what was said, rather than why it was said.

Collec (Collectivism)

Collec culture emphasizes the ingroup, such as the organization or the extended family. Collecs value harmony and avoid direct confrontation. They emphasize building relationships with others through rituals and politeness, and task accomplishment becomes an indirect or secondary goal. Each individual represents the group to which he or she belongs, so if an individual is hurt, the group is hurt; if an individual is helped, the group is helped; if an individual is shamed, the group is shamed. The communication style is typically indirect.

Let us look at an interview with a Collec client where the interviewer does not do a good job of giving feedback.

Interviewer:	Hi there! What can I do for you (she walks around the desk to meet the guest)?
Collec:	Hello (stands in the door somewhat startled by the direct approach).
Interviewer:	It's good to see you alone so we can talk confidentially and without distraction.
Collec:	Oh (long pause). We were not sure why you wanted to see me when you asked me to come here.
Interviewer:	Well, let's get down to business, then (shuffling papers on the desk). Why do you think you deserve subsidized housing?
Collec:	(pause) Would it be all right if I came back later and brought my brother with me (backs up toward the door)?
Interviewer:	You seem very anxious. Are you afraid to ask or are you uncertain about your reasons for applying?
Collec:	Excuse me, but I really have to get back home. We'll give you a call (avoiding eye contact).

The interviewer takes a very direct approach with this client almost immediately and makes the client feel isolated. The interviewer interprets the client's discomfort as the client's possibly being unworthy of services. The client responds with embarrassed silence and prefers to end the interview. The interviewer is not aware of her role in increasing the client's anxiety.

Let's look at a second interview between an interviewer and a Collec client with a more successful outcome.

Interviewer: (stands as the client enters the room and smiles) Welcome! Good to see you. I hope your family is well? Let's move over to the comfortable chairs (motions toward the two upholstered side chairs). May I fix you some tea or coffee?

Collec: No, thank you. Our family is all well, thank you for asking. We are fortunate to have you as our family friend.

Interviewer: It is my privilege to be included among your friends. Your family is well known and respected in our community.

Collec: It is always relaxing to come here. You always seem as though you had all the time in the world to sit with one of us.

Interviewer: Many good people here help me get the work done.

Collec: If it would not be too much trouble, we would like to hear your opinion on a situation facing our family (he looks down, not smiling).

Interviewer: (sits attentively and quietly in polite silence waiting for the client to begin)

The interviewer shows respect to the client and the client's family and expresses interest in them, valuing the client through his ingroup. Offering a comfortable side chair and a hot drink are symbols of friendship and harmony for the relationship and of hospitality for an honored guest. The interviewer emphasizes that he, the client, is not an isolated individual. The silence provides the client with an opportunity to think through what to say next without feeling pressured.

Dialogues: Hierarchy Dimension

Hipow (Large Power Distance)

Hipow culture emphasizes the unequal distribution of power in institutions and organizations in a hierarchy of privilege. A few people have a lot of power; the vast majority has little. Power is experienced as a personal attribute, something to be felt rather than enforced. Hipows will usually be quiet, soft-spoken, and polite, whether they are powerful individuals or not, but if they feel that you are being unfriendly or uncaring, they will be silent. Hipows will show their trust in you by asking for help and direction and will show their respect by remaining formal and lowering their eyes. When Hipows make direct eye contact or do not display positive and animated nonverbal behavior, you have probably hurt or insulted them and have lost their respect. Hipows will not hesitate to talk but will be restrained and formal in their conversation, seeking to please you as best they can and accepting blame for any failure to please you. While they will internalize stress, they will give indirect signs of their stress in their interaction with you. Two simulated interviews where the interviewer is not necessarily in a position of power over a Hipow client will illustrate these patterns.

Power is experienced as a personal attribute, something to be felt rather than enforced.

Interviewer:	(enters the room) You seem to be unhappy. Can you tell me what's troubling you (looking directly at the client)?
Hipow:	I am fine, thank you (sitting down but looking away).
Interviewer:	Are you angry with me?
Hipow:	(silence)
Interviewer:	You need to become more open with your feelings or we can never improve our working relationship.

Hipow:	I am sorry that I cannot do that (looking at the interviewer directly).
Interviewer:	I'll be able to help you change if you will let me.
Hipow:	I am sorry that you are so unhappy with me (looking out the window).
Interviewer:	You don't seem to be paying attention to me. Are you angry with me right now?
Hipow:	(sits silently, continuing to look out the window)

It is clear that the interviewer acted inappropriately with this Hipow client by focusing on inferences rather than observations and by making judgments. From the start the interviewer was utterly insensitive to the Hipow culture's indirect ways of giving feedback, however polite, which indicated a negative reaction. When the interviewer kept pressuring the client, this reaction deepened into unfriendliness, distrust, disgust, and boredom. While the Hipow client had to remain respectful and accept blame for any problems that occurred, the lack of trust and respect made any positive outcome from the feedback very unlikely.

It may be useful to examine a second example with a Hipow client. This conversation has a successful outcome.

Interviewer:	(enters the room) You seem quiet today. Would it be appropriate for me to ask if something is bothering you?
Hipow:	It is very kind of you to ask (looking downward).
Interviewer:	(after a period of silence) When another colleague of mine had a problem, I was able to help solve it.
Hipow:	That was good. I know about that person (nodding in agreement).

Interviewer:	Caring about others is a good thing, like an older brother for a younger brother (eyes lowered and speaking quietly).
Hipow:	Perhaps you will have the time to listen to my thinking about my younger brother.
Interviewer:	You do me great honor by asking me.
Hipow:	It is difficult for me to speak with outsiders about this thing.
Interviewer:	Sometimes being an outsider can be an advantage if the outsider cares about you.
Hipow:	Yes, that is true, and I do believe you care.

Here the rules for providing feedback were followed. The interviewer focused on gaining the client's trust, on not being judgmental, and on not presuming to give advice or to push the client faster than desired. The interview also demonstrated cultural awareness by following the client's lead in being soft-spoken and polite, allowing the client to ask for help with a sense of safety and reducing the threat by speaking indirectly rather than directly to or about the client. The use of silence and supportive nonverbal behavior was also helpful. Bringing in the hierarchy of family relationships also helped the client accept the outsider interviewer in a respectful and appropriate role.

Lopow (Small Power Distance)

Lopow culture values horizontal relationships where everyone is on a level playing field. Status symbols and privilege invite ridicule, and those who would set themselves above others are cut down to size. While a boss has power and authority, he or she must be careful to respect workers and share the benefits of that power whenever possible. Everyone is expected to have a voice in decision making, and each person or group has rights and feels free to complain when those rights are violated. There is a strong sense of what is fair, and when workers sense they

are being treated unfairly, they feel free to complain and negotiate to improve their situation.

Let us look at an example of an interviewer behaving inappropriately with a Lopow client.

Interviewer: (speaking on the phone) Yes, please show
the man in. I will see him now.

Lopow: (saunters in, dressed casually and looking
around the office) Hi. Good to see you again.

Interviewer: (somewhat put off by the casual manner,
looking directly at the client but not rising
from his chair) Can I help you with something?

Lopow: Maybe yes...maybe no. We'll see (sits down
uninvited in one of the comfortable side
chairs). Maybe I can help you (smiling at interviewer)!

Interviewer: I'm not sure what you mean (he looks frustrated and stern). You made the appoint-
ment—you must want something.

Lopow: Perhaps that was a mistake. You seem terri-
bly busy right now...(looking out the win-
dow and sitting in awkward silence with both
hands in his pockets).

Interviewer: You're right. I am very busy. I would appreciate your getting on with whatever you came
to see me about.

Lopow: (smiles and begins to clean his fingernails)

The interviewer, intentionally or not, has several protective lay-
ers, such as the receptionist, his office, and his desk, between
himself and the Lopow client. The interviewer values the status
of his position and sees his behavior as appropriate for that
status, regardless of what the Lopow client might think or feel.
The Lopow client assumes a deliberately informal style and
enjoys teasing the interviewer. Each unintentionally but quickly

insults the other, and their conflict becomes personal and de-structive.

It might be useful to look at an interview with a Lopow client that has a successful outcome.

Interviewer:	(she approaches the visitor) Glad you could make it. Come on in to the office so we can talk.
Lopow:	Hi. Yes, let's talk (saunters into the room beside the interviewer).
Interviewer:	Good to see you again, catch up on how you're doing, and all that. I've heard good things from your mates about how well the group is working together (sits down in a comfortable chair, offers the other chair to the client, and pours a cup of tea for both).
Lopow:	Yeah, we're not doing so bad. We do our share (smiling and leaning back with his legs crossed).
Interviewer:	You never let us know how well you're do-ing, do you? We've really got to keep an eye on you guys (laughing)!
Lopow:	We make sure we get our share, that's for sure. We'll take you on any time you take advantage (laughing also).
Interviewer:	So what can I do you for (smiling and taking out a pad of paper and pen)?

The interviewer goes out of her way to equalize the relation-ship with the client, downplaying the obvious status symbols of her office and authority role. She shows interest and gives praise in an appropriate manner. There is friendliness and a give-and-take, half-joking exchange between the two. The in-terviewer shows respect and a willingness to take seriously what the client has to say.

Mascus emphasize assertiveness, masculinity, money, and material things rather than nurturance, quality of life, or the needs of others.

Dialogues: Gender Dimension

Mascu (Masculine)

Mascus emphasize assertiveness, masculinity, money, and material things rather than nurturance, quality of life, or the needs of others. This holds for both males and females, though the trait is much more obvious in males. Mascus treat life as a competition. They believe themselves deserving and destined to excel—by force if necessary. To Mascus, power means power to make others do what you want them to. Mascus like to show off by being the biggest, best, and fastest there is. They are expected to flirt and like to be noticed when they come into the room. They like to dominate discussions and to compete, especially when there is a chance of winning. The males in particular like sports, often roughhouse with other males, and love to use sports metaphors. Mascus tend to argue and criticize others, even when they do not intend to be antagonistic. They look up to heroes and look down on losers.

Let us look at an example of an interviewer using techniques that are unsuccessful with a Mascu client.

Interviewer:	I'm glad you came to me for help. Please sit down over there (he indicates a chair across the desk).
Mascu:	(taking a different chair beside the interviewer) Well, I'm not glad. Let me tell you! I don't want to be here one little bit!
Interviewer:	You certainly seem frazzled. I've never seen you so upset (leaning far back in the chair and looking at a file).
Mascu:	Hey, Mac! Look at me! I just passed you the ball and you fumbled it. You gotta pay attention if you're going to win the game.
Interviewer:	You think we're playing a game here? You think I'm playing against you or something?
Mascu:	Everybody plays. Just catch the ball when I pass it, and feed off to me so I can shoot!

Interviewer:	I haven't a clue what you're talking about, but you sure seem like you are having a good time here at my expense. What's the big idea?
Mascu:	(he looks out the window, not saying anything)

The interviewer kept the client at a distance and tried to impose an agenda on the client, and the client didn't like it. The two started competing for power in the interview, and soon found themselves at a dead end. The interviewer was not comfortable with the sports metaphors the client preferred to use and perceived the client to be a loser. The client resented the implied put-down. He quickly lost interest in the interview and gave up on the interviewer as a source of help. The interviewer got angry with the client and erred by focusing on the person rather than the person's behavior and by making ungrounded inferences and value judgments about the client. The interviewer was uncomfortable and defensive, focusing more on his own needs than on those of the client.

Let's now examine an interview where the interviewer is more skilled in interacting with a Mascu client.

Interviewer:	How's it going? Come on in and sit over here by me, so we can talk together (shakes his hand and leads the client to two chairs close together). You want some coffee or anything?
Mascu:	(takes a chair) No, thanks…but thanks for askin'. It's a bummer. I'm not feeling so good right now.
Interviewer:	Yeah, you look kinda hurtin'. I'm used to seeing you up there fightin' back and winning the game!
Mascu:	(smiling and shaking his head) Not today. No way! I've got problems. Maybe even you can't help me (looking directly at the interviewer).
Interviewer:	Give it a shot. We're on the same team here. What's the problem?

Mascu:	I'm gettin' bad grades and havin' a hard time at school with the teachers.
Interviewer:	You're used to winning and now you're afraid of losing? Is that it?
Mascu:	Yeah…I wish it were just a ball game. I know how to win there…but this academic stuff…that's something else.
Interviewer:	Maybe some of the same things you use to win ball games can help you with the academics. Let's get a handle on things here and talk about what needs to be done so you can feel better. Okay?

The interviewer here seems much more comfortable with the client in the client's own frame of reference, using sports and competitive metaphors and helping reinforce the client's self-esteem. The interviewer does not avoid physical contact and lets the client direct the conversation toward his own stated goals and objectives. The client's strengths are emphasized, and the challenge of being successful in academics is presented in terms he is likely to understand. The interviewer also grounds every inference and observation in specific client behaviors, avoiding value judgments and focusing on the here and now. The interviewer works with the client by sharing information rather than giving advice and by focusing on the client's needs rather than the interviewer's own agenda.

Femi (Feminine)

Femi culture expects both males and females to be cooperative and nurturing in their relationships. They are supposed to be sensitive to the needs of the disadvantaged and are quick to offer help to those who need it. Modest, they downplay their accomplishments or power in society and depend on soft negotiation and compromise rather than forcing a conclusion by confrontation. Saying how good you are is called bragging and is considered very unacceptable. Small talk is a favorite pastime. Femis value the feelings of others as important to a relationship. It is playing that matters, not winning.

Let us look at an example of an interviewer whose style is unsuccessful with a Femi client.

Femi: Good morning (he stands at the door).

Interviewer: One moment (she does not look up and keeps working).

Femi: (after a pause) Excuse me, but I think we were supposed to have a meeting.

Interviewer: Yes, okay! What is it then?

Femi: Well, I wondered…you know, it's been a year since my last performance evaluation….

Interviewer: Yeah. You're doing a great job. Wish all men were like you (smiling mischievously at Femi)!

Femi: (not smiling)…so I thought perhaps…(looks at a chair but does not sit).

Interviewer: (makes inviting gesture) Sure! Go ahead!

Femi: …well…if you might consider…

Interviewer: Listen, don't waste my time. You came to see me, so say what you have to say.

Femi: (looking hard at interviewer) It's really no use talking to you! You are so full of yourself (walks off)!

The Femi client intends to ask for a raise in pay—something a Femi does not do easily. He is put off repeatedly by the interviewer's behavior. First she is not prepared for the interview, then she flirts with him, does not invite him to sit down, and does not meet him halfway in what he wants to say. In fact he expected her to suggest the pay raise herself, which he felt was obviously what he was hinting at with his hesitant phrases. When instead of giving him her full attention the interviewer starts pushing him, he releases his frustration.

Femis value the feelings of others as important to a relationship.

Now let's look at an example where the interviewer is more successful.

Interviewer:	Hello there, glad you found the time to stop by (he shakes her hand and guides her toward the office, both smiling). No problems getting here?
Femi:	None, thank you. It was easy to find the place.
Interviewer:	Good.
Femi:	Thank you for scheduling this meeting. I have heard good things about you from others (as both move to the side chairs and seat themselves).
Interviewer:	(obviously pleased by the positive remark) Oh, it's just my work, you know. I hope we can come up with some helpful ideas (looking seriously concerned and sympathetic).
Femi:	Yes (showing obvious relief and leaning back in her seat).
Interviewer:	It's going to be difficult for me to make changes, and I will need your help so we can avoid losing money for the company. By working together I am sure we can make it happen.
Femi:	I've figured out a plan that might work. Your suggestions will help me modify the plan so it will work even better (showing papers and taking a businesslike attitude).
Interviewer:	Looks good! You've done your homework! I really appreciate your willingness to look at this situation from our viewpoint.
Femi:	No problem (showing relief in her smile).

The interviewer takes the Femi client seriously and treats her, both verbally and nonverbally, with gentleness and modesty from the first point of contact. The interviewer is very careful not to impose the power of his status on the client; he respects her viewpoint and lets her determine the pace of the conversation.

Dialogues: Truth Dimension

Uncavo (Strong Uncertainty Avoidance)

Uncavos have no tolerance for ambiguity. They like a safe, predictable world. When they are friendly, they will respond in detail, being formal and unambiguous. When they are unfriendly, they become vague in their responses and seek to end the interview. If they trust you, they will debate and argue heatedly from either side of a polarized right/wrong, good/bad position, seeking to find the truth through argument. If they distrust you, they will be openly critical and challenge your credentials directly. They show interest by being very task oriented and by asking many questions. They prefer direct eye contact. If they become bored, they will be passive and look away. They are good speakers, well organized, and verbal though sometimes loud. Their gestures are animated, but they avoid physical contact. They have rigid beliefs that do not change easily, which often causes them to quickly, and sometimes prematurely, evaluate a situation to separate right from wrong.

They have rigid beliefs that do not change easily, which often causes them to quickly, and sometimes prematurely, evaluate a situation to separate right from wrong.

Here is an interview that quickly turns sour because the interviewer uses the wrong style with an Uncavo client.

Interviewer: So, how do you want to begin?

Uncavo: You're the interviewer. You tell me.

Interviewer: I thought that maybe you would have an idea of what you wanted to talk about (he looks away from the client).

Uncavo: I want to know what to do so that I don't fail in my duty and responsibilities. I want you to tell me.

Interviewer: That's an interesting insight. Maybe you want me to help you explore different solutions to your problem?

Uncavo:	You keep trying to change the subject as though you don't want to tell me the truth (waving arms to demonstrate frustration). I don't think you know what I should do. I don't think you are doing a very good job here!
Interviewer:	You seem angry with me. We'll have to work together if we're going to solve your problems. I don't really know what the best answer is, but maybe we could explore possibilities.
Uncavo:	If you don't know or won't tell me what I should do, then why in the world am I wasting my time here (gets up)?
Interviewer:	Please, don't get so emotional. Try to relax (also stands up and reaches over to pat the client on his back).
Uncavo:	Don't you touch me (leaves the room)!

The interviewer constantly avoids being directive when the client wants the interviewer to tell him what to do. The interviewer is trying to consult with the client as a coparticipant, which the client interprets as indecision or weakness. The client begins to form an opinion of the interviewer as incompetent and challenges him. When the interviewer tries to redirect the client's anger toward the problem, the client becomes more frustrated. The interviewer is judged as indecisive and weak and his admission of not knowing answers becomes the final straw for the client, who ends the interview. The interviewer's overfamiliar attempted pat on the Uncavo's back puts the "crowning touch" to the disastrous interview.

Let us look at a second example of interviewing an Uncavo client that is satisfactory to both.

Interviewer:	Please sit down over there, and I'll sit down here.
Uncavo:	I need to know what I'm doing wrong and why I feel as I do.

Interviewer:	Tell me the three most important feelings that seem to be bothering you.
Uncavo:	Let's see…I feel I'm not being as responsible to my duties as I should be…I feel insecure and sort of anxious…and I need more structure to do the right thing (looking directly at the interviewer).
Interviewer:	First, we will look at your perception of not being responsible regarding your duties. Which specific duties are a problem?
Uncavo:	My wife and children don't obey me.
Interviewer:	So, one of your problems relates to obedience and order in your family life. Before we concentrate on that problem, let's look at the second problem you mentioned. You said you were feeling insecure and anxious. Why?
Uncavo:	I always feel a little anxious. Right now I need to know what to do with my wife and children so that my home can be a sure and certain refuge for our whole family and we can go back to a regular routine again.
Interviewer:	So you want me to tell you how to restore order to your family so it can return to the routine it once had where everybody knew their role and did what was expected of them. Is that accurate?
Uncavo:	Yes, that's it exactly (smiling and nodding his head vigorously).
Interviewer:	And the third problem you mentioned was not knowing exactly what to do next. You want a map or plan for what you should do to guarantee success. Is that right?
Uncavo:	Exactly! That is precisely what I want. Do you think you can help me (looking directly at the interviewer)?

<table>
<tr><td>Interviewer:</td><td>Okay. Let's begin by analyzing each part of the situation. By your telling me the details, we can identify first, what went wrong, second, why it went wrong, and third, what you need to do to fix it.</td></tr>
</table>

In this interview, the interviewer provided a great deal more structure. The interviewer recognized the client's initial concern and responded in a rational series of steps to construct a clear agenda for proceeding, using the three statements made by the client. As a result the client was willing to be more detailed and task oriented in responding. The interviewer also demonstrated good feedback technique by focusing on the person's behavior, by detailing observations without making inferences, by refraining from judging the client, by focusing on what was being said rather than why, and by attending to the client's rather than the interviewer's needs.

Unctol (Weak Uncertainty Avoidance)

There is a tendency to avoid setting rigid rules and laws but to resolve any conflict that might arise.

Unctols take life easy. They tolerate and even celebrate ambiguous situations; the more unfamiliar the challenge, the greater the adventure. There is a tendency to avoid setting rigid rules and laws but to resolve any conflict that might arise. There is an easygoing attitude toward structure and schedules along with a tendency to "wing it," to work out solutions to problems on the spur of the moment. Unctols tolerate very different behaviors and avoid conformity whenever possible. They believe in common sense and feel that formal protocols are for stupid people.

Let's look at an interview with an Unctol where the interviewer is utterly insensitive to the client's cultural style.

<table>
<tr><td>Interviewer:</td><td>Glad you got here on time (not smiling).</td></tr>
<tr><td>Unctol:</td><td>Yeah, last time I had something going on…I couldn't get away. Sorry to disappoint you by being on time (smiles to indicate it's a joke).</td></tr>
<tr><td>Interviewer:</td><td>Please sit down in that chair and let us not waste any time joking (not smiling).</td></tr>
</table>

Unctol:	Hey, relax man, it's bad for your health to work too hard (smiling pleasantly and joking in tone).
Interviewer:	You're impossible (unsmiling and getting angry)! When are you going to grow up anyway?
Unctol:	Oh, come on, my friend. This is your turf. Just let me know how I can fit in.
Interviewer:	I am sorry. Until you take things more seriously, there is nothing for us to talk about. Come back later when you are more ready (clearly angry).

The interviewer was clearly upset with the Unctol client even before the interview, from at least one previous visit when he felt insulted by the client's not being on time. He was looking for an excuse to get angry and create an incident. The client was being playful and not trying to offend, but the results were judged offensive nonetheless. The client now probably considers the interviewer to be an overworked nervous wreck.

Now here comes a more successful interview.

Interviewer:	How's it going? You taking care of business these days (joking, friendly tone and presence while she guides the client into the office)?
Unctol:	Could be worse. No complaints here. How about you (moving casually toward the side chairs and both sitting down in a relaxing way)?
Interviewer:	Ah, you never get very bothered by anything, do you?
Unctol:	If you say so, it must be true (smiling and serving himself tea).
Interviewer:	What kinds of adventures do you have in mind for us today? You are always full of surprises (laughing and getting out paper and pen).

Unctol:	It's always a challenge to surprise you. You are ready for most everything, but this time I have a beauty for you (smiling with pride and anticipation).
Interviewer:	Okay, I'm ready for you. Let me have it (smiling but picking up the pen to take notes)!

The interviewer and client interact playfully as they get down to business and get ready to go to work. The joking serves to clear the air and establish a context of friendliness between them. The interviewer allows the client to set the rules of procedure without imposing her authority. The problem is viewed by both as a positive challenge to their ability to work together creatively.

Dialogues: Virtue Dimension

Lotor (Long-Term Orientation)

Members of the Lotor culture take a long-term perspective on life, longer than their own life span. Living a virtuous life in the eyes of their ancestors and providing for their children are vital to them. They are determined and never give up their responsibility, although they might compromise the methods by which they achieve those end goals. They work extremely hard. It is being prosperous that counts, not being happy. They tend to be unceremonious and to keep a low profile.

It is being prosperous that counts, not being happy.

Let's look at an interview that does not go well with a Lotor client.

Lotor:	I've got some ideas for a solution to that problem of ours, but I need your help to make things work. Can you help me (respectful and careful in approaching the interviewer)?
Interviewer:	Hello, my friend! Nice to see you again. Is your mother any better?
Lotor:	Yes, thank you. But I need your help (shows the interviewer the notes in her hand).

Interviewer:	You know, I think I saw you in the street yesterday.
Lotor:	Is that so?
Interviewer:	Yes, with two other persons. You were going shopping, it seemed.
Lotor:	Oh! I am so stupid. I forgot about a meeting I have. Please excuse me (leaves).

The interviewer means to be warm and chatty to put the visitor at ease and then get down to work. But the client misinterprets the interviewer's attempts at small talk as lack of commitment and grows more and more frustrated. Not wishing to damage the relationship, she first attempts to get back to her question, then to be evasive, and finally she contrives a credible excuse—another duty—and leaves frustrated. The interviewer never realizes this and just wonders about this silly person walking in and out of the office.

Now let's look at an interview that goes better.

Lotor:	I've got some ideas for a solution to that problem of ours, but I need your help to make things work. Can you help me (respectful and careful in approaching the interviewer)?
Interviewer:	I'll bet you've got some good ideas, and we can both try to make them work (smiling as he guides both to the side chairs).
Lotor:	Thank you. I've done a careful job of putting this solution together, but without your help all that work will be wasted.
Interviewer:	Let's get to work, but as you know, this will take some time. We'll probably need several meetings. We don't want to try a simplistic solution to this complex problem, right (looking up for an answer)?
Lotor:	Absolutely right! Let me show you some notes I put together and get your opinion

(takes out papers with numbers and lays them out in front of the interviewer).

The interviewer shows respect for the client and respect for the ideas that the client is presenting. The common ground between interviewer and client is well defined and reinforced by both. The respect both have for the complexity of the problem, and therefore the proposed solution, is also obvious and becomes part of the common ground. Both parties have a commitment to stay the course for as long as it takes.

Shotor (Short-Term Orientation)

Shotors are eager to live for the moment and to show immediate results. Traditions are unquestionably important. Much time is spent in social ritual for its own sake. Reciprocating gifts is a moral obligation, even if it means incurring debts. Shotors are not driven by goals but by a desire to show personal stability. They smile, are pleasant, and like to socialize. They celebrate whenever they have the chance. If you have Shotor friends, though, make sure never to cause them to lose face.

Let's look at a failed interview with a Shotor client.

Shotors are not driven by goals but by a desire to show personal stability.

Shotor:	Hello! How are you today?
Interviewer:	Hello. I am glad you came by. I was just going to call you about some problems we have been having.
Shotor:	Oh? Why did you want to see me?
Interviewer:	I'm afraid your group is not meeting its obligation, and the future investments of the company are potentially at risk (she looks stern).
Shotor:	What do you mean? Our bottom line was up 25 percent this quarter!
Interviewer:	I'm talking about the five-year plan.
Shotor:	Five years is a long time. It's no use getting worked up over that now.

Interviewer:	We are an ongoing business. The world does not stop turning today, you know.
Shotor:	So right (he sits down but glares out the window).

The client begins in what he considers an appropriate way, expecting an outgoing, friendly exchange. The interviewer disregards this, and she immediately makes him lose face by accusing his group of not measuring up. The client is incredulous and stung by the criticism but tries to maintain composure and not make the interviewer lose face. Things go rapidly downhill from there. The two talk past one another. By the end, the hostility between them is obvious and will thwart any meaningful dialogue they might have in the future.

Let's look at a successful interview with a Shotor client.

Shotor:	Hello! How are you today?
Interviewer:	(she stands up to meet the client) Fine, as always when I see you! Have a seat.
Shotor:	Thanks (he sits down).
Interviewer	(also sits down) I wonder if you could help me with my problem.
Shotor:	Of course! We can talk about it. What did you have in mind?
Interviewer:	Some of the students in your group are making trouble. I know they hold you in high esteem, so your help would be much appreciated.
Shotor:	Sure, I can bring them into line. No problem. I'll go and talk to them right now. What happened?
Interviewer:	I'll tell you. Oh, first before I forget, remember that other problem we talked about last week? I am taking care of it.
Shotor:	Good! I knew I could count on you.
Interviewer:	So the problem is….

The interviewer starts by reciprocating the client's preference for a warm exchange and shows respect by standing up and letting the client sit down first. She also shows regard for the client's face by asking for his help and mentioning how he is held in high esteem among the students. The interviewer also confirms that she is doing something for the client in exchange for this help, making this a reciprocal exchange.

Conclusion

The basic message of this chapter is that even a well-intentioned interviewer can cause the interview to fail if he or she has no appreciation for the communication preferences of the client. Some communication behaviors are appropriate in all cultures, but many are not.

In all cultures an interviewer should demonstrate an interest in the client, should listen, and should pay due respect. The client should feel valued and at ease as a result. If an interviewer does not demonstrate interest and respect, the interview is almost certainly going to be a failure. But even if the interviewer has the best intentions, he or she has to know how to behave in such a way that the client perceives these good intentions. These behaviors are culturally determined.

Consulting, interviewing, or counseling that ignores the cultural context is unlikely to be accurate and appropriate, except to impose the will and rules of a more powerful group on less powerful groups in the short term. Cross-cultural consulting, interviewing, and counseling are presented here as obvious and practical contexts for communicating adequately in a world of culturally different peoples.

In all cultures an interviewer should demonstrate an interest in the client, should listen, and should pay due respect.

Chapter 6

Summing Up

It is now time to take stock of what you have learned so far in this book. Let us return to the six statements with which we started (see page xvii) and see whether you have revised your thinking about them. We authors have added to each of the statements some comments that represent our viewpoints.

- The world is essentially a global village.

    In a village the locals understand one another with a nod, a joke, a gesture. Our global village, despite airlines and satellites, is a far cry from that. Thanks to transport and communication technology, individuals from all over the world can now—if they have the means—meet and form meaningful relations or conduct profitable trade. But groups of people still commonly perceive other groups of people as uncivilized, and there are no signs that this is changing any time soon. Yes, there are global marketplaces in our world, but these are not at the center of a snug global village.

Groups of people still commonly perceive other groups of people as uncivilized, and there are no signs that this is changing any time soon.

- The world would be a better place if everybody behaved like the people in my country.

    This is precisely the tacit assumption in much of popular wisdom, journalism, and political rhetoric about international issues. In some cases it is even overtly asserted, for instance in the concept of the "rogue state" that we met in the account of The Frankfurt Incident.

If one uses the moral standards of one culture to judge another culture, that other culture will invariably appear to be morally inferior.

What we have shown in this book is that if one uses the moral standards of one culture to judge another culture, that other culture will invariably appear to be morally inferior. This holds for major, nationwide issues just as it does for everyday behaviors. If all peoples maintain that their ways are the best, this is not going to make the world any better. We do feel that the world urgently needs moral discourse across countries in order to cope with the large and small problems facing us. But such a discourse quickly becomes a quarrel, or even a war, if one starts by proclaiming one's own country to be morally superior. The first step should be to try to understand why the others act as they do and to recognize that from their perspective their actions make sense.

- One could live in any country in the world if one is honest and well intentioned.

  This is a sympathetic but unrealistic statement. Even in a country with only nice people (if such a place existed), the statement would not hold. Many of the stories in this book show how, despite the best intentions, people can insult other people through misunderstandings across cultures. Whether in employment, in peaceful negotiation, in friendship, or in war, messages that are sent across cultural boundaries can only be correctly interpreted if the receiver appreciates the cultural context from which these messages were sent. Without cross-cultural understanding trade will suffer, personal relationships will suffer, and wars will escalate.

- Business is business in any country.

  This statement is about as true as the following ones: "An individual is an individual in any country," "A leader is a leader in any country," "A woman is a woman in any country," "A man is a man in any country," "The truth is the truth in any country," "Virtue is virtue in any country." Yes, business exists in every country, just as individuals, leaders, women, men, truth, and virtue exist there. But business is a different game with different rules in each country, and here is what we predict: this will still be the case many years from now, when technologies will be much more advanced than they are now, and when the word *globalization* will have gone out of fashion.

- Children's upbringing at home and their lives in school and later in the workplace are unrelated.

As the spectrum of examples in this book indicates, the five dimensions of culture are manifested across all social situations. This is obviously true in countries where a totalitarian regime holds a tight grip on home, school, and the workplace. But it is no less true in an anarchic or democratic society. All people in that society are continually adjusting their behaviors to remain in tune with the vast chorus of voices in that society. Children imitate their parents and later their teachers and their classmates. Followers imitate their leaders and bosses. Producers try to please their customers. Leaders try to please their electorate. Journalists and playwrights try to please their audience. Thus, national culture continually re-creates itself in social interaction.

- National cultures will be a thing of the past fifty years from now and beyond.

There are now some six billion people in our world, almost all of whom have a very special relationship with their country. The majority of babies born today are taught from early on to love their country. A multitude of symbols and rituals serve to instill this love firmly in their minds: they are taught to respect their country's flag, to sing their country's national anthem, to be proud of their country, and to despise certain other countries. Many of them are taught to be prepared to die for their country. How will these people think and act fifty years from now, when their generation rules the world? Will they love all countries in the world with equal fervor? Will they brandish a world flag and sing a world anthem, and in which lan-

Business is a different game with different rules in each country.

National culture continually re-creates itself in social interaction.

The world will not have become one village in fifty years, neither at the level of symbols and rituals nor at the deeper level of values.

guage? To us this is merely a rhetorical question. The world will not have become one village in fifty years, neither at the level of symbols and rituals nor at the deeper level of values.

Clearly we authors disagree with all six statements. This does not make us pessimistic. The current ease of exposure to foreign cultures in much of the world is an opportunity for learning as well as for creating problems. People have learned new tricks in the past, and they can do so in the future. The ability to communicate across cultures more effectively needs to be one of them.

If you apply the things that you have learned in this book, you can start contributing to better cross-cultural understanding. To summarize, we shall use the familiar steps of building awareness, knowledge and skills.

Awareness

You have learned, through many stories and exercises, that people from different countries usually have different social rules. If you communicate with people from other countries without knowing those differences, you will very likely misattribute at least some aspects of their behavior. You will find meaning where none was intended, or you will miss meaning where it was intended. You will feel that the foreigner has strange, rude habits. You will react emotionally by feeling puzzled, angry, or frustrated. The exchange is likely to be a failure in the sense that you will not obtain the result that you intended, and you will have negative expectations about interacting with people from that part of the world in the future.

There are always many factors in addition to culture that contribute to a particular course of events.

On the other side, you are aware that not all behaviors can be explained through national culture. There are always many factors in addition to culture that contribute to a particular course of events. These include personalities of people involved, things that happened in the recent past, and other factors. You have also learned that cultural differences that are not national but are regional or ethnic could be at play. Differences in national culture are only one of the explanations for what happens in any interaction.

Knowledge

You have learned that national culture is what distinguishes the people in one country from those in another. The differences among societies can be summarized in five overarching dimensions of culture. Three of them are about relations between people:

1. *Identity*, about relations between self and groups

2. *Hierarchy*, about relations between powerful and less powerful individuals

3. *Gender*, about relations between men and women

The two others have to do with what is and what should be:

4. *Truth*, about one eternal truth versus many context-dependent truths

5. *Virtue*, about doing what is right here and now versus preparing for the future

You have conceptualized each of these five dimensions as a continuum:

1. Collectivism—Individualism

2. Large power distance—Small power distance

3. Feminine—Masculine

4. Strong uncertainty avoidance—Weak uncertainty avoidance

5. Long-term orientation—Short-term orientation

You have learned that every society has its own orientation regarding each of these five dimensions. You have worked with the synthetic cultures as a means to isolate each dimension from the other four, and to see how that dimension affects social interaction.

Skills

By practicing the ten synthetic cultures you have acquainted yourself with both extremes of all five dimensions of culture. This gives you a better idea of what to expect when communicating with real people in real foreign countries. The book should in particular prepare you for surprises. There are no simple recipes for communicating across cultures. Listening carefully and being constantly aware that your own frame of reference may not be sufficient to make sense of what you see and hear are essential skills.

Conclusion

In addition to awareness, knowledge, and skills, chapter 1 mentioned *will* as a prerequisite for cross-cultural learning. Extending your frame of reference, with which you have lived from infancy, is both intellectually and emotionally challenging. But if you have read this far, you most certainly have the will to learn! We hope you will find occasion to practice what you have learned so far and that you will experience the joy of discovering new worlds and making new friends.

Part III
Group Work and Simulations

Chapter 7

Group Work for Cross-Cultural Learning

This chapter presents the idea of simulating cross-cultural encounters. We set the scene through some initial group acculturation exercises, including role playing. Then we progress to what we call the Synthetic Culture Laboratory. The laboratory is a framework for practicing the synthetic cultures in teams made up of the different synthetic cultures and interacting over a situation of their choice. A sample situation called "Troubles with Outsiders" is presented. The Synthetic Culture Laboratory moves us into the realm of simulation gaming, that is, a social activity with its own rules that is carried out for the purpose of experience-based learning, but where the rules of the activity also simulate some aspect of social reality.

Framework for Group Work

All structured work needs a framework. Cross-cultural learning is no exception. We have defined culture as the rules of the social game. Culture has to do not with people's personalities, but with how they expect each other to act in social contexts. People who share the same culture play the social game by the same rules. People from different cultures, however, play by different rules and often appear ill-bred because they break the rules of proper conduct that one's group is accustomed to. Loss of trust is often the result.

People who share the same culture play the social game by the same rules. People from different cultures, however, play by different rules.

The point of intercultural group encounters is to learn to interpret the behavior of cultural others accurately. This is crucial to successful cross-cultural communication. A person's behavior only becomes meaningful when it is connected to the culturally learned expectations that led to that behavior; in other words, to the rules of the game. A culture-aware approach seeks to interpret behavior by placing it within the context of culturally learned expectations and values, by identifying the cultural rules, and by learning how those rules translate into behavior. Group exercises and simulation gaming have long track records as successful ways of teaching behavioral skills.

Here is a suggested general framework for using this book with a group of participants.

1. Prepare participants for the topic of cross-cultural learning by giving them chapters 1 and 2 to work on (2-4 hours of work). Discuss the learning.

2. Prepare learners for working with the synthetic cultures by giving them the synthetic culture profiles, exercises, and sample dialogues to read. This involves chapters 3 to 5 and will take another 2-4 hours of work. Discuss the learning in class.

3. In a plenary session, conduct group exercises with the synthetic cultures and debrief them. Use the acculturation exercises found here in chapter 7. This will take 2-4 hours.

4. Run a simulation. Depending on the audience, use one of the formats given in this part of the book, or create a simulation of your own. In either case, use chapter 8 to prepare for the session. The actual simulation might take 1 to 4 hours. It is usually followed immediately by the next step.

5. Debrief the simulation. This is where you tie the simulation experiences back to the learners' real lives and where you have to draw lessons at the level of awareness, knowledge, or skills. You can use chapter 6 to sum up the lessons that your learners can derive, depending on their level of ambition. You can return to chapter 2 to revisit the five

Group exercises and simulation gaming have long track records as successful ways of teaching behavioral skills.

basic problems that constitute the five dimensions. This session can take about as much time as the simulation itself.

6. If possible, consolidate the learning. There might be weeks or months between the previous step and this one. You can use chapter 2 to recapitulate the five-dimension framework, and the learners might now have their own cross-cultural experiences to bring to the meeting and discuss. This could take between 2 hours and a full day.

The synthetic culture acculturation exercises that follow allow you to practice synthetic cultures in three activities that are less structured than in Parts I and II. They encourage participants to be more creative with the cultures and are easy to facilitate.

Synthetic Culture Acculturation Exercises

Find Favorite Words

Ask participants to try to think of three more favorite words to add to the list of words that carry a positive connotation in each of the ten synthetic cultures. These words can be adjectives, nouns, or verbs. (Ask participants to go back to chapter 3, where the synthetic culture profiles are presented.) Then form small groups and instruct participants to compare lists. Next, bring the entire group together and ask each group to report its words and explain how each word fits the synthetic culture for which it was selected. It may be helpful to keep running lists of the ten cultures on a whiteboard or on newsprint to avoid duplication.

You might find that the same word could fit several different cultures. For example, *leader* might fit both a Hipow and a Mascu culture, or *considerate* might fit Collec and Femi equally well. Note, however, that these words do not mean exactly the same thing in the two cultures they apply to. Their meaning is derived from the cultural context. In a Hipow culture, for example, leaders are born, whereas in a Mascu culture, they are self-made. In a Collec culture, one is supposed to be considerate to ingroup members, whereas in a Femi culture, one should be considerate to everyone, particularly to the poor and the weak.

Flashes

Ask everybody to write down a brief cross-cultural exchange from their own experience and then interpret it from the point of view of various synthetic cultures. Act out some of the exchanges, with participants playing different synthetic culture roles. Short, informal discussions will follow. The objective is to see how the same behavior by one person can be interpreted altogether differently by another person, depending on that person's synthetic culture.

If no incidents from the participants' experience are forthcoming, here are some possible ones:

- A father or mother comes home from work.

- A teacher enters the classroom.

- You are queuing at the counter in a shop and somebody behind you asks you if he or she can go first.

- At closing time, a colleague asks you to go for a drink.

- Two people try to get through a narrow doorway simultaneously.

- A car bumps into the back of your car without causing physical damage.

Role Playing

Participants act out conflict-prone situations by playing the roles as though they belong to synthetic cultures. The content can be adapted from current topics in the news or in the participants' organizations. Groups and teams can work simultaneously, or one group might role-play while the others observe.

We suggest that you start the role playing with single-culture teams. Several teams can act out the same incident in parallel with differing synthetic cultures. To make things more complicated—and more realistic—mix the teams up so that you now have teams made up of different synthetic cultures acting out the same situations together.

Allow ample time for debriefing. Typically, debriefing these short role plays takes up to twice as much time as the role playing itself. Here are some suggestions for topics. Adjust or revise them to fit the group, and supply the details as appropriate, for example, with actual proposals or projects.

- Decide about writing a research proposal. Money has become available for a $1,000,000 grant on research related to health needs. The group (each member in a different synthetic culture role) needs to reach unanimous agreement to receive the money.

- Project budget allocations. A five-year and ten-year plan for the organization is being discussed and budget allocations are being projected.

- Plan or evaluate a project. A project (pick an actual project) is being evaluated by a group to decide whether to proceed with the project.

- Launch an international marketing campaign. First, have a team devise the campaign. Create actual drawings, slogans, or video clip storyboards. Then ask locals from a number of foreign countries to comment.

- Hire a person for a job. To get started, assemble two stacks of identical personnel folders to select from. After each interviewer and each interviewee have had time to peruse the contents of his or her folder, these participants can role-play human relations staff and job candidates from different synthetic cultures who meet for a job interview.

Almost any business decision becomes a simulation when those making that decision are in their synthetic culture roles. Here are some more brief suggestions.

- Conduct a performance appraisal.
- Evaluate a product from the point of view of the users.
- Welcome a VIP.

The role plays can also take place in a nonbusiness context:

- Discuss a topic at a "town meeting."
- Take a personality test, first as yourself and then "in role," as an anonymous member of your synthetic culture.
- Run a committee meeting on an actual problem but with the participants role-playing their synthetic roles.
- Have a party (birthday, New Year's Eve, or other).
- Plan a trip.
- Get stuck in an elevator together.
- Your town has just experienced a major natural disaster. Have a meeting to discuss recovery efforts.

The Synthetic Culture Laboratory is not actually a simulation but rather a framework for creating discussions in synthetic culture roles.

The Synthetic Culture Laboratory

In the original Synthetic Culture Laboratory (Pedersen and Ivey 1993), four synthetic cultures are used, each taken from a different dimension of national culture. The synthetic cultures of Hipow (large power distance), Uncavo (strong uncertainty avoidance), Indiv (high individualism), and Mascu (strong masculinity) provide four one-dimensional stereotyped perspectives based on one end of four dimensions of national culture.

Any combinations of synthetic cultures can be used, depending on the audience, without changing the overall idea.

Basic Data

Objectives: To simulate cross-cultural discussion on any topic

Target audience: Any collection of people with an interest in the subject matter

Preparation time for participants: None

Briefing and setup time: 15 minutes

Playing time: 1 to 4 hours

Debriefing time: 15 minutes to 4 hours

Number of players: 8 to 50

Materials required for players: Handout "Troubles with Outsiders" or any other case description you choose (see pages 182–84)

Materials required for facilitator: Briefing and debriefing instructions

Equipment/room setup required: Room for group briefing and debriefing and one breakout room for each host culture

Description

In the Synthetic Culture Laboratory, from two to ten host cultures representing the chosen synthetic cultures interact with teams of visiting consultants from each of these synthetic cultures. Depending on the particular objective, you can vary two parameters:

1. The particular synthetic cultures used. All ten can be used in any combination you consider appropriate.

2. The problem situation that serves as the content matter of the laboratory. This situation should be taken from the context of the participants' experience. It can be any problem situation that requires group interaction.

Rules of Play

The first step is to assemble your group. As few as eight (with four persons to two synthetic culture groups) or as many as about fifty (with the synthetic culture groups varying in size but with none smaller than four persons) can participate. Divide the group into teams representing the desired number of synthetic cultures. The second step is selecting a synthetic culture. The participants may be assigned to particular synthetic cultures, determined by the facilitator's objectives, or they may be allowed to choose one culture. If you decide to run the simulation with participants assigned to a culture, you may want to give each participant only the rules for his or her own synthetic culture (see chapter 3). If participants choose their own synthetic culture, each participant will first be given the rules for all synthetic cultures. From our experience we have found that the laboratory seems to work best when participants know as much as they want to know about all synthetic cultures and then are allowed to select a synthetic culture for themselves.

Then follows the third step, which is to instruct each group to socialize within its new synthetic culture. First they will go over the guidelines together. After the participants read about their new culture, they will be expected to ask questions and interact with one another using the beliefs and behaviors of their synthetic culture. They could use exercises from chapter 4 to get them started. Usually thirty minutes is sufficient for participants to learn the beliefs and behaviors of their new synthetic culture identity.

The fourth step is to have the participants engage in a problem-solving assignment. This assignment *must be the same* for all the teams. It must be carefully crafted in advance and relevant to participants' experience. The problem needs to satisfy the following conditions:

- that it take between thirty minutes and two hours to solve, and
- that it require teamwork.

This step will take approximately fifteen minutes, enough to get teams working on the assignment but not enough to finish it. One assignment that has worked well in the past consists of having participants identify the problems that have resulted from "outsiders" coming into their synthetic home culture community from the other synthetic cultures. Based on the values of their home synthetic culture, the participants should be able to identify at least ten negative effects of this inmigration of outsiders. The handout "Troubles with Outsiders" is located on pages 182–84 and includes descriptions for all ten synthetic cultures.

The fifth step is to select teams of two or more consultants from each synthetic culture to be sent to one of the other synthetic cultures to help them solve the problem that is posed by the assignment. The selection of consultants may be included as part of step three or four.

The sixth step is for each synthetic culture to send its team of two consultants to another host culture. The consultant teams will be allowed from ten to fifteen minutes to help the host culture solve the problem. The team of consultants and the host culture persons are instructed to stay in their synthetic culture roles during the consultation but also to seek common ground across cultural boundaries.

At the end of the ten or fifteen minutes, consultants and participants are instructed to discard their synthetic culture roles and to discuss the interaction within their groups for five to ten minutes. What worked and what did not work and why? What did they learn about the synthetic cultures, about each other, and about themselves that might be useful in working with real-world cultures?

Next, as the seventh step, the consultant teams report to their "home" cultures on what they learned, and the home culture members report on what they learned from their visiting consultants. After about ten minutes of debriefing, each synthetic culture is instructed to send its consultants for a visit to another host culture. The sixth and seventh steps are now repeated with the other cultures as many times as there are cultures to visit or as time permits.

The eighth step is for a representative from each synthetic culture to report back to the larger group on (1) what the group learned about their own synthetic culture, (2) what they learned about the other synthetic cultures, and (3) what they learned about themselves that might be helpful in working with real-world cultures.

The final step is your debriefing of the exercise, during which you point out some of the cultural patterns and other insights gained from observing the teams in action.

Debriefing

Here is a list of questions that you might want to consider as you debrief the Synthetic Culture Laboratory.

1. Were you able to discover elements of the different synthetic cultures in your own real behavior? If so, give examples.

2. Can you remember conflicts in your community between groups that were emphasizing different synthetic culture perspectives? If so, give examples.

3. Were you able to find common ground with any of the other synthetic cultures without giving up your own in-

tegrity and/or forcing the members of the other synthetic culture to give up their integrity?

4. What feedback do you have for members of each of the other synthetic culture groups in terms of things you liked and did not like about their synthetic culture?

5. What advice do you have for outsiders who come into your synthetic culture group that will help them find common ground?

6. Did you notice an increase in your skill for finding common ground as you progressed through each round with a different synthetic culture group?

7. Did you as consultants feel a sense of "coming home" each time you returned to your synthetic culture to prepare for the next round?

8. Did you feel a sense of disorientation as you encountered members of the other synthetic cultures?

9. Do you have a better understanding of why groups from different cultures might have difficulty working together?

10. (for those who chose their synthetic cultures) How did you decide which synthetic culture to join, and why? If you were going to participate in another laboratory, which culture would you select?

Variations

When the workshop group is small, rather than send out consultants, instruct all the members of one group to visit all the members of each of the other groups in turn. In each round, then, each synthetic culture team meets one other team. The entire group spends ten minutes role-playing a problem-solving session, acting within the rules of their synthetic cultures. Then follow the nine-step procedure above.

Once a class or workshop group has become familiar with its own synthetic culture, it is possible to set up a variety of situations for training cross-cultural interviewers. Some of these possibilities might be as follows:

- Develop a group including persons from all synthetic cultures and role-play a group counseling experience or a problem-based work team or committee.

- Assign interviewers who are not familiar with any of the synthetic cultures to role-play a group or individual counseling interview with clients from your choice of synthetic cultures; similarly assign a trainer who is not familiar with the synthetic cultures to facilitate a discussion about time management with a group from a chosen synthetic culture.

- Discuss the same problem in separate synthetic culture groups to identify an appropriate approach for dealing with that problem, then report that finding to the larger group. If the group is not unwieldy, ask them to identify an approach for solving the problem that takes into account the various viewpoints of all of the synthetic cultures represented.

- Discuss a problem in the entire group with participants from your choice of synthetic cultures, responding in role to one another during the discussion, or videotape any of the above exercises and debrief the group by discussing it.

Troubles with Outsiders

The following descriptions provide examples of problems that each synthetic culture (e.g., Indiv) is experiencing with temporary/permanent visitors from other synthetic cultures. As we mentioned earlier, other problems can be substituted to fit the interests and needs of the participants. The more specific and locally relevant the problem, the more constructive the discussion and the more useful the laboratory experience.

Indiv

Outsiders are holding us back by failing to behave like everybody else. They need to integrate and disperse into our society, not huddle together, doing obscure business without paying taxes. Let them learn our language and come to our shops, schools, and clubs. What are they waiting for? They smile, but they are secretive and devious. If they do not want to mix with us, what did they come here for?

Collec

How can people be so rude and blunt? Outsiders without even the rudiments of manners come in and act like they own the place. They live a lonely, utterly opportunistic life. They talk about things they know nothing about but never listen properly. We are tired of being exploited by some of these visitors and their companies who take advantage of our hospitality to make lots of money, then send that money outside our community. Although we work for them, they do not take care of us. We helped them, so they should help us and our families.

Hipow

These visitors have no dignity. They speak when they should be silent. They do not know their place. It is impossible to know who to talk to because they all act like they are the leader. Besides, these people disregard our traditions and history as though they did not matter. Some come into our community to "help" us with all sorts of new ideas, values, and "things" that undermine the authority of our traditional leaders.

Lopow

Some outsiders have no mouth and others have no ears, it seems. The first category is not too much trouble, unless you want them to take some initiative. And they never look you in the eye, either. The second category is worse. We are tired of having visitors come into our community and set themselves up as better than the rest of us. We make fun of them when we can, but they have no sense of humor. It's like these visitors think they have all the answers. They don't know what it means to be fair.

Mascu

It's like every loser in the world comes here to take advantage of our success without paying their dues. We don't mind accepting visitors who are willing to help us out, but we don't like those who live out of our pockets. Our economy depends on taking advantage of opportunities that bring in the big bucks. Those outsiders don't want to do any work. All they do is whimper about every little thing. We need to escort those losers out of town ASAP.

Femi

It is hard to imagine how insensitive these outsiders are to the needs of others. All they care about is competition and fighting. It's no wonder their kids bring knives to school. The men are macho, and the women look like dolls and act phony. They obviously come from unloving, alienated societies. We need to help them if we can.

Uncavo

These outsiders wander around without direction, but not us. We know what we stand for, and those beliefs weld together the structures of our society. People who disregard our laws and customs are a threat and a danger to us, whether they know it or not. They look strange, and who knows what crimes and obscure business they are engaged in. Let them stay in their own depraved countries and not bring their immoral way of life to us!

Unctol

Life is for living. Those uptight visitors who try to impose rules and barriers to fence off their little corner annoy us. We have a good life here, with little stress, and we have done well enough. Now the visitors bring stress and anger into our community with their ready-made answers and their intolerance. They keep on talking even after we have stopped listening. I wish they would relax.

Lotor

Those visitors who want easy answers to hard questions will destroy our community if we let them. They come in and promise the earth to us, but we cannot rely on them. They are here and gone. They have big parties and big plans and leave behind only a mess that we have to clean up. They have no honor, no sense of duty or purpose. If we are not careful, we will end up mortgaging our futures and the futures of our children to these people.

Shotor

Some of these visitors don't let us get close to them; they keep everyone at a distance in a very unfriendly way. We have the feeling that they are always busy with their own ulterior motives, even when we are doing our best to help them. They are penny-pinching in their social support. Most of all they have no respect for tradition, and they do not know how to entertain visitors. Real bores!

Chapter 8

Using Synthetic Cultures in Simulations

Playing by different rules without knowing it is a basic element of games and simulations about intercultural encounters. Such simulations often generate uncomfortable feelings or confusion, even anger, that feel a lot like the frustration that real intercultural encounters can generate. But it is preferable to experience this frustration during a simulation and learn from it than to experience a misunderstanding or even a confrontation in a real-world setting and do damage to relationships.

Simulations on the Market

Simulation games about intercultural encounters have existed for many years. In this section we shall present a few types of simulations by discussing a well-known example of each. This paves the way for introducing the concept of synthetic culture simulations.

After NAFTA

One can incorporate realistic national cultural characteristics in role profiles as was done, for example, in *After NAFTA: A Cross-Cultural Negotiation Exercise.** This simulation uses cul-

One can incorporate realistic national cultural characteristics in role profiles.

---

* Butler, J. K., et al. (1996) "After NAFTA: A Cross-Cultural Negotiation Exercise," in *Simulation & Gaming: An International Journal* 27, no. 4, 507–16.

tural role profiles based on three of the dimensions of national culture defined by Geert Hofstede. It involves negotiations between the mayors of two fictitious towns on the Mexico-U.S. border. The subject at stake is the location for a new plant. The Mexican mayor has a brief cultural script for large power distance, collectivism, and uncertainty avoidance. The script for the U.S. mayor is from the opposite ends of these three dimensions. According to the author, the simulation can lead to synergy but also "poses myriad problems relating to cross-cultural misinterpretation, misevaluation, and miscommunication." This, he adds, makes it very challenging and interesting but difficult to debrief.

BaFá BaFá

Many existing, full-fledged simulation games employ more elaborate systems of rules. Probably the most well known of these is *BaFá BaFá*, created by R. Garry Shirts in 1977 and available through Simulation Training Systems (www.stsintl.com/business/bafa.html). This simulation has been run innumerable times around the world. It works best with approximately twenty to thirty participants, who are divided into two groups, the "Alpha culture" and the "Beta culture." The two groups have widely different sets of "cultural" rules. The Alpha culture is relationship-oriented, hierarchical, and collectivist; social rituals are of prime importance. The Beta culture is a highly competitive, individualist trading culture. The participants learn the rules of their own cultures and begin practicing them. After some time, observers visit each others' cultures and engage in social interaction. These visits result in misperception, misinterpretation, and emotions that simulate culture shock. Understanding the misunderstandings becomes the aim of the debriefing.

For most participants, playing *BaFá BaFá* is a very emotional experience. Just like in real intercultural encounters, outward similarities hide significant differences. For instance, both the Alpha and the Beta cultures have a practice of exchanging cards, but the meaning of this practice is entirely different in

Just like in real intercultural encounters, outward similarities hide significant differences.

EXPLORING CULTURE

the two cultures. A foreign visitor will miss this point because of surface familiarity with the card-exchange practice.

The intense culture clash that *BaFá BaFá*, or any other culture clash game, generates does not necessarily lead to better intercultural understanding. If the experience conflicts with strong convictions held by participants, they may refuse to invest in it or learn from it. We must add that a skillful facilitator can overcome many problems and still achieve learning. Preparing and debriefing the participants is particularly important for allowing them to make sense of the experience.

Barnga

The simplest way to simulate an intercultural encounter is to take the idea of different rules literally and have players play a game where they have different rule sets, but without being aware of it. This idea is used in the game of *Barnga* that was created by Sivasailam Thiagarajan and Barbara Steinwachs (1990). This game is available through Intercultural Press (www.interculturalpress.com/shop/barngatext.html).

Players start playing a card game, "Five Tricks." Players sit around tables in small groups and each player tries to win as many "tricks," or rounds of play, as possible, according to the rules. Once the players have learned the rules, they are not allowed to speak anymore. After five minutes or so of play, the winner and loser (taker of the most and fewest tricks) change tables. Without being aware of it, players soon find themselves at a table with other players whose rules are minimally different. It doesn't take long before several players think that the same trick should rightfully be theirs to collect. This of course leads to a variety of responses. Players may feel that others are cheating, or they may feel confused or frustrated at not knowing what is happening. Occasionally a player may become angry and even refuse to play anymore. Only a few players will get the idea that, actually, the others don't have the same set of rules. Even so, they may not know how to resolve this situation, because they aren't allowed to talk—like not being able to

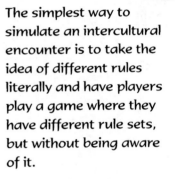

The simplest way to simulate an intercultural encounter is to take the idea of different rules literally and have players play a game where they have different rule sets, but without being aware of it.

speak the language of the other players. Because the basis for this confusion and frustration is so evident and so simple and yet the feeling of disorientation is so similar to the disorientation stage of culture shock, *Barnga* is a very powerful game. Also, it is easy to point out in the debriefing that one set of rules is not intrinsically better than another.

Different-rule games such as *Barnga* are a far cry from reality, but they work very well because they are so simple and straightforward.

The objective is to simulate real workplace situations more closely.

Ecotonos

Ecotonos: A Multicultural Problem-Solving Simulation follows a pattern similar to *BaFá BaFá* but its objective is to simulate real workplace situations more closely. The simulation was created by Nipporica Associates and Dianne Hofner Saphiere (1997) and is available through Intercultural Press (www.intercultural press.com/shop/ecotonostext.html). It has been conducted in a number of languages and across many professions.

The simulation works best with twelve to fifty participants, but it has been run successfully with much larger groups. Participants are divided into three fictitious cultural groups: Aquila, Delphinus, and Zante. These cultures operate according to "culture rule cards," chosen by the facilitator to simulate real-life cross-cultural differences. There are ten types of rule cards for each of ten characteristics such as leadership, teamwork, gestures, listening styles, and problem solving. Each type of card has three variations representing a position with regard to one of these characteristics. For example, variations in decision-making preferences include consensus, democratic, and autocratic. All teams get one of the variations for three to four cultural characteristics so that each team has a different cultural script.

The simulation proceeds in three stages. First, each team gets some time to discuss its cultural rules and to create a myth about its origins (for the purpose of practicing their rules). Then all teams get the same task or case study to work on. This could be a physical or an intellectual task, a business-oriented or a committee-oriented case, depending on the objectives of the session. When the participants are well into working on their task, groups are recombined in such a way that each team consists of players from all three cultures, in different proportions, to simulate joint-venture, majority-minority, and multicultural teams. These newly formed teams then continue to work on the same problem, but now bringing to the task three different sets of cultural characteristics.

Ecotonos has the merit of being very flexible in the choice of culture scripts and tasks. Culture scripts have purposely been kept very simple. They bear no direct relationship to existing national cultures. *Ecotonos* can be used more than once with the same group, always with different results; it can thus be used to measure intercultural learning.

Randömia Balloon Factory

Randömia Balloon Factory: A Unique Simulation for Working across the Cultural Divide is similar to *Ecotonos* in that its objective is to simulate a realistic situation in a business context. In *Randömia*, Western trainers (composed of some mixture of U.S. Americans, Anglo-Canadians, British, Irish, Germans, and others who are culturally direct, individualistic, egalitarian, and assertive) from the country of Richland attempt to train workers in a manufacturing plant in the Third World (Randömia) to achieve greater efficiency and product quality. The plant employees are culturally indirect, collectivist, harmonious, and hierarchical—characteristics that are shared among many nonindustrialized countries. The training fails, of course.

The actual simulation takes place two days after the training, when the Richlanders try their best to find out what went wrong and, not surprisingly, are unable to. When they ask the Randömian employees what happened, they get only polite and positive feedback. Trapped in their cultural armor, the Richlanders apply the same tactics for the interviews that they

One unique feature of the simulation is that the Richlanders play themselves.

would use at home. They can't see that their behavior might be part of the problem, nor can they even imagine how they might approach the Randömians differently.

One unique feature of the simulation is that the Richlanders play themselves (the reason for the makeup of the Richlander group); they are not assigned cultural roles as are the Randömians. The result of the interaction between these two opposite cultural groups is frustration and confusion, the feelings that often occur when people from different cultures come together. Although this is one of the simulation's best features, the requirement of a specific cultural mix for the Richlanders can also be a drawback. Without the required nationalities (in whatever proportion), the simulation won't work.

Randömia is designed for fifteen to thirty-five participants and takes approximately three hours. The debriefing section is thorough and well designed. *Randömia* was created in 2001 by Cornelius Grove and Willa Hallowell, partners in an intercultural consulting firm for corporate clients. *Randömia* is available through Intercultural Press (www.interculturalpress.com/shop/Randomiatext.html).

In summary, it is fairly easy to incorporate elementary culture clash into a game or simulation, as *Barnga* demonstrates. To go beyond that is more difficult. The ultimate aim of cross-cultural simulation gaming is to help people see exactly what goes wrong in cross-cultural encounters and what they can do to prevent it; in other words, to improve people's skills in intercultural communication. These aims are elusive for two reasons. First, as the experiences with *Bafá Bafá* illustrate, it is difficult not to evaluate other cultures as being less sensible than one's own. Second, real national cultures are so rich and multifaceted and they interact with personalities and situational contexts in so many ways that one can hardly ever directly point a finger at culture's consequences. This is what causes the "myriad problems" in debriefing *After NAFTA*.

EXPLORING CULTURE

The ideal cross-cultural simulation would deal with both problems. It would demonstrate that one culture is not intrinsically better than another, and it would not be too complex for the participants to make sense of their experiences.

In order to find a suitable level of complexity, amenable both to realistic simulation and to rational analysis, the synthetic culture approach has been developed.

The Synthetic Culture Approach to Simulations

Synthetic cultures provide a temporary laboratory in which cross-cultural communication skills can be safely nurtured and developed for transfer later to real-world contexts.

Synthetic cultures, as we have learned, embody aspects of real-world national cultures in ten extreme-case stereotyped alternatives (see chapters 2 and 3 for a review). Paul Pedersen and Allen Ivey (1993) coined the term *synthetic culture* and created the first four synthetic cultures. These have since played an important part in training consultants, counselors, and interviewers through the means of role playing, case studies, critical incidents, and other activities. Synthetic cultures provide a temporary laboratory in which cross-cultural communication skills can be safely nurtured and developed for transfer later to real-world contexts.

There are countless ways in which to use the synthetic cultures. So far, we have introduced and presented a large number of individually oriented activities, several group exercises, and the Synthetic Culture Laboratory. We have reviewed several commercially available simulation games and are ready now to turn our attention to simulations employing synthetic cultures.

As you will remember from your earlier reading and practice, it takes three steps to acquire cross-cultural competence: awareness, knowledge, and skills. The first step in developing cross-cultural communication skills is to become aware of the existence of culturally learned assumptions, or "mental software," in ourselves and in others. Frequently, those assumptions are so unconscious that we overlook them. They filter our comprehension of reality. The synthetic cultures allow the participants to rehearse the process of discovering their own culturally learned assumptions.

The second step in developing cross-cultural skills is to increase our knowledge about particular cultures. The synthetic culture environment allows the trainee to learn about how the many different cultures and countries see the same issue differently—or don't see the issue at all.

The third step in developing cross-cultural competence is to acquire actual skills in interacting with different cultures. Skills that are grounded in an appropriate awareness and accurate knowledge are most likely to be effective in multicultural situations.

Why Synthetic Cultures?

There are several advantages to using synthetic cultures for developing cross-cultural skills. Here is a list of the merits of synthetic cultures.

1. *Empirical grounding*. The synthetic culture model is, as we have learned, based on the authoritative experimental evidence from Geert Hofstede's research. Hofstede's work links the synthetic cultures (via his five cultural dimensions) to the value systems of over fifty countries. Because the extreme tendency demonstrated in each synthetic culture was derived from data about real-world cultures, learning about and practicing synthetic cultural patterns are relevant in preparing persons to work with actual cultures. The five-dimensional framework and its ten derived extremes (synthetic cultures) provide people with a model for organizing their experience in contrasting actual cultures. They learn to identify the elements of all synthetic cultures that present themselves in greater or lesser amounts in every encounter with a new or unfamiliar cultural group.

2. *Personalized learning*. The synthetic culture approach involves participants in ten contrasting cultures, making the learning more personalized than would an abstract discussion about cultural differences or similarities. Participants learn to articulate viewpoints from "inside" the contrasting cultural perspectives.

3. *Completeness*. Synthetic cultures create a microcosm of cultural variability for examining the same issue from multiple real-world viewpoints. The synthetic cultures repre-

sent the world's predominant cultural identities in a caricatured form. Also, there is usually enough variation among participants within each synthetic culture group (resulting from their own nationality, ethnicity, religion, age, gender, socioeconomic status, lifestyle, and other affiliations) to ensure that each participant's interpretation of his or her synthetic culture role will be slightly different, just as in reality.

4. *Safety*. Because no synthetic culture replicates any particular real-world culture, role-playing them and dealing with them are less risky than with real-world cultures. The consequences of conflict among synthetic culture players in a training setting are less likely to violate the sensitivities of participants than are those of real-world identities that are simulated in activities such as *After NAFTA*. If, for example, a particular culture, country, or ethnic group were directly judged, any resulting conflict or disagreement might carry over into the actual relationships among participants and thus increase risk levels.

5. *Stereotyped value patterns*. People tend to apply their cultural values unthinkingly when they react to social stimuli. By exposing participants to stereotyped synthetic cultures, trainers may be able to help them avoid applying those stereotypes in the real world. Once they recognize the extreme forms depicted in synthetic cultures, participants may be better able to recognize and deal with less extreme forms in actual cross-cultural encounters.

6. *Separating behaviors from expectations*. The synthetic culture approach creates an opportunity for participants to learn that in a cross-cultural encounter, one cannot assume that behavior exhibited by one's foreign interlocutor expresses the expectations that one is used to in one's home culture. In other words, across cultures the same behavior might be linked to different expectations, or different behaviors might be linked to similar expectations.

EXPLORING CULTURE

7. *Creation of room for common ground.* When persons from a variety of real-world cultural backgrounds are brought together into the same Synthetic Culture Laboratory experience, those different people temporarily share the same cultural "home" perspective. It becomes possible for people to discover other shared characteristics across cultures without having to give up their actual, real-world identities.

8. *Self-examination.* By temporarily taking on the new identity of a synthetic culture, people gain insights into unexamined assumptions about their own cultural patterns. These assumptions are tested as participants hear themselves talk in their synthetic culture roles. Dissonance is created wherever conflict between the synthetic and actual cultural identity occurs, resulting in participant self-examination.

9. *Symmetry.* The synthetic culture model is symmetrical. It does as much justice to one extreme of each of the five dimensions of culture as it does to the other extreme. Thus the model gives a nonbiased overview of the cultural spectrum that exists among the world's societies.

10. *Analytical strength.* The synthetic culture model isolates each cultural dimension from the other four. This makes synthetic cultures much simpler to debrief than real cultures would be. They provide examples of cultural values derived from real cultures but without their overwhelming complexity. Learning to deal with the limited complexity of synthetic cultures provides the basis for learning about the much more complicated cultures of the real world. The synthetic culture rules are complex enough to challenge participants but not to overwhelm them. It takes ten minutes to read a synthetic culture profile well and twenty more to become reasonably competent at role-playing it. The complex task of developing awareness, knowledge, and skills is nurtured in working with synthetic cultures.

Culture is rather like the color of your eyes; you cannot change it or hide it, and although you cannot see it yourself, it is always visible to other people when you interact with them.

How to Role-play the Synthetic Culture Profiles

It is crucial for the players in a synthetic culture exercise to realize that culture is not something like a coat that you can choose to either wear or hang on the wall. Nor is it like your hairdo that you can change by going to the hairdresser or wearing a wig. Instead, culture is rather like the color of your eyes; you cannot change it or hide it, and although you cannot see it yourself, it is always visible to other people when you interact with them. This is how players should consider the synthetic cultures; their culture profile pervades everything they do.

So the synthetic culture profile determines not only how players will talk to players from other synthetic cultures during a meeting but also how they walk, how they open the door and whether they close it, how they use the space in a room, whether they smile, how they greet one another, whether they look at one another or touch, how they say good-bye at the end of a meeting, and so on.

In the same vein, the culture profiles apply no matter what the context of the simulation is. Many simulations are set in business or workplace contexts, but the synthetic cultures apply just the same in family, classroom, or holiday contexts, mutatis mutandis.

Finally, cultural rules are always a matter of pride. People take pride in their culture and in its rules. They take pride in being decent, well-behaved citizens of their country or region. When participants role-play a synthetic culture, they must try to feel this pride and to enjoy it.

To play a synthetic culture well requires considerable emotional investment because culture is so deeply rooted, and it is so challenging to have to enact values that are not one's own. But it is also a very rewarding experience, and one that is necessary to improve one's cross-cultural understanding and competence.

Selecting Synthetic Cultures for Your Simulation

Selecting a good mix of synthetic cultures is an important consideration. If you plan to use a synthetic culture simulation as a general-purpose introduction to cross-cultural communication, you will want to spread a broad base by introducing and role-playing all ten synthetic cultures. If you don't have enough participants for ten teams, choose one profile from each dimension. In the latter case, choose profiles that are remote from the value orientations of most of your group members.

If you are working with employees of larger institutions, take note: the issues that most often cause friction between institutions from different countries are *hierarchy* and *truth*. This implies that Hipow/Lopow and Uncavo/Unctol might be good synthetic cultures to choose.

If you are working with people who will be living for some time among foreigners, then the issues of identity (Indiv/Collec), gender (Mascu/Femi), and virtue (Lotor/Shotor) take precedence.

In general, Western cultures are more concerned with truth (Uncavo/Unctol), whereas Asian cultures are more concerned with virtue (Lotor/Shotor). If you have a group of people from these two parts of the world, you may want to include these two dimensions.

If you have participants from two specific countries, consider selecting only the synthetic cultures for the dimensions in which the two countries differ most. For instance, if you have Japanese and Americans for participants, it makes sense to include Indiv/Collec, Uncavo/Unctol, and Lotor/Shotor, since Japan and the United States differ greatly on these dimensions.

Of course these are no more than a few pointers. Each training program has its own specific situation.

Changing the Profiles

The synthetic culture profiles presented in this book are set forth in a format that is directly usable for gaming. In some cases you may find it desirable to abbreviate them or to add elements that better suit the context of the simulation. One of the simulations discussed later in this book, *Follow-the-Sun Global Technology Team* (see chapter 10), provides an example of both simplifying and adding to three of the synthetic cultures.

You may even wish to combine synthetic culture profiles to obtain multidimensional profiles. This, too, is a valid adaptation. Keep in mind, however, that multiple profiles add significantly to the complexity of interpretation and debriefing and require high levels of knowledge and experience from both players and facilitators. Our suggestion is that if you wish to work with multiple profiles, facilitate single-dimension synthetic culture simulations with a group first.

Because of the flexibility of the synthetic culture profiles, you can quite easily add them to an existing simulation, for example in the areas of international business or negotiation. In fact, for most experienced trainers, this is probably the most practical way to use synthetic cultures. Obviously, adding a synthetic culture to a simulation with which you are unfamiliar adds to the complexity of the exercise.

Because of the flexibility of the synthetic culture profiles, you can quite easily add them to an existing simulation.

Selecting and Preparing for a Simulation

Selecting the right simulation for a particular group can be a difficult task. Here are three questions we think you should consider in order to choose an appropriate simulation.

First, what do you want to achieve by conducting a simulation? Is it only to make the participants aware of the variety of cultural differences in the world and to demonstrate that these differences can create misunderstandings? Is it to impart knowledge of one or more of the culture dimensions? Or does your audience need specific skills to communicate with people from

What do you want to achieve by conducting a simulation?

specific cultures? Your level of ambition, the needs of your audience, and the amount of time you have will help determine the type of simulation or simulations that best suit your purpose. As an indication, you might need an hour to create awareness through a few simple synthetic culture acculturation exercises, an entire day to build knowledge through a synthetic culture simulation with a thorough debriefing, and a month if you aim for culture-specific skills, which require not only simulated experience but real-world practice as well.

Second, who is your audience? For instance, if you have a group of young students from one country with very little cross-cultural experience, you cannot expect to achieve more than a beginning level of awareness. For such a group, select a few group acculturation activities, the Synthetic Culture Laboratory, or a very simple simulation.

Who is your audience?

If your audience is from a specific professional sector and your aims are also related to that sector, you may want to run an exercise with content matter taken from that same sector and adapt it for synthetic cultures. In this case the Lab may be ideal because of the ease of adapting the problem. The complexity of the content matter and the synthetic cultures themselves compete for the participants' attention. If you choose a full simulation that is both enthralling and complex, participants may forget about their synthetic culture profiles.

If all participants are from the same country, they may not take the concept of synthetic culture very seriously because they won't see the profiles as relating to real life. It becomes easy for them to revert to their normal behavior patterns during the simulation. This can make your job during the debriefing a nightmare. If participants can listen to those from other countries or to those with mixed-culture personal histories comment on how the experience with synthetic cultures relates to their own life, this will help.

Third, how much time is available? Quite often a simulation leader has high ambitions but lacks the time to fulfill them. A typical "solution" is to cut back on the time for introducing and debriefing the simulation. Although the experience may

How much time is available?

still be enjoyable, this is a recipe for poor learning. If you find yourself in such a time bind, we suggest that you choose a group exercise from chapter 7, introduce it well so that the participants know the objective of the exercise, and debrief it thoroughly so that the participants can relate their experiences to their real lives. A rule of thumb is that you should spend no less than 20 percent of the time you have available on introducing a simulation and no less than 30 percent of the time on debriefing. If 10 percent of the time is needed for plenary start-up, this leaves roughly 40 percent of the time for playing the simulation.

One other important matter to settle before the day of the simulation is how you will create teams. You may have an obvious rationale for team composition, for example, if you have groups of participants from different locations or organizations. If there is no built-in rationale, start by letting the players choose their synthetic culture, a strategy that increases their motivation. If players choose a synthetic culture that differs from their own value on that particular dimension, their role playing becomes more deliberate, and they are likely to learn more during the simulation. If you let participants choose their synthetic culture, this choice can be the basis for teaming up. Pick the specific synthetic cultures you want to include, then let the participants choose their culture while space is available.

If the participants know one another, their personal histories might come into play. It could occur that participants use the simulation setting to settle personal accounts. This will hinder debriefing.

Having a group of homogeneous young people in a simulation is not ideal. They tend to be preoccupied with their identities and relationships. This inhibits their role playing. Our advice here is to prepare the participants even more thoroughly than you would otherwise. Also, when you choose teams, distribute clusters of friends across teams to prevent teams from becoming cliques.

Another matter concerns the role of observers. In a large group some persons will typically prefer to be observers rather than take part in the simulation. Letting such participants be observers will prevent their being put in an anxiety-producing situation. On the other hand, players may become more self-conscious if observers are present. To solve this dilemma, instruct the participants to form teams first and then choose their own observer. The observer will take part in the acculturation of the team but will not participate during the simulation. Observers should be asked to listen actively during the simulation and participate during the debriefing; they often bring valuable and unique perspectives to the discussion.

If possible, provide for attractive symbolic prizes for winning teams; it makes the simulation more fun and increases players' emotional investment. Offer two prizes: one for the team that wins from the simulation world's point of view and a "synthetic culture award" for the team that most convincingly enacts its synthetic culture.

Introducing the Simulation

Adequately introducing the aim(s) of the simulation is of crucial importance for success. Be clear, enthusiastic, and brief. Tell the participants *why* they are doing this simulation, *how* it works, and *what* roles there are.

We have found it useful to explain to participants that although the synthetic cultures are entirely fictitious, the five social issues they address are real and are developed from empirical evidence, and the clashes that result from playing them are very realistic. This means that although the participants are not playing people from any real country, they will be experiencing *feelings* very much like those which they might feel when encountering people from other cultures. Make the point that different social rules are at the heart of differences between cultures.

Although the participants are not playing people from any real country, they will be experiencing feelings very much like those which they might feel when encountering people from other cultures.

Practicing the Synthetic Cultures

The participants typically have some anxiety when they assemble for a simulation. The simulation leader's first job is to help the

The participants typically have some anxiety when they assemble for a simulation. The simulation leader's first job is to help the participants relax through acculturation exercises.

participants relax through acculturation exercises (see chapter 7). Once the ice has been broken, the atmosphere changes and becomes playful. Teams will need to practice to get comfortable with their new set of values, to get a feel for their synthetic culture without having to perform a demanding task at the same time. The Synthetic Culture Laboratory, with an actual problem facing the group, will get the group members discussing and interacting in their synthetic culture roles. Picking a hot problem not only makes the task more immediately relevant to the different cultural perspectives, it also makes applicability to the synthetic culture roles more practical for the participants than a fictitious problem would.

Another way to get participants to feel comfortable with their synthetic culture roles is to have each team introduce itself to the others "in role." Just like in normal life, the teams will not talk explicitly about their synthetic culture, but their culture will show in the way they present themselves.

Anxious Participants

If during the preliminary acculturation exercises some participants show marked signs of anxiety (for example, asking questions about the roles they have to play or being silent and withdrawn), you, as the simulation leader, need to be able to identify the reluctance and to offer them a way out. One such way out, as we've mentioned earlier, is as observers within their team. This gives them an opportunity to avoid role playing without losing face. If possible, a better solution is to try to answer their concerns and to reassure them.

Some groups may be more likely to feel anxious than others. A participant may, for example, be the only one from his or her country or may have difficulty with the language. Also, participants from some countries are more likely to be anxious than others. People from collectivist countries, for instance, are likely to feel very insecure at breaking the boundaries of their ingroups. To them, the idea that group affiliation is something that one can change for the duration of a game is foreign. In countries with strict rules for behavior—often associated with large power distance and strong uncertainty avoidance—it is much harder for somebody to play at being somebody else than in countries with low power distance and strong uncertainty tolerance, particularly if there are significant status differences among the participants. You could try pointing out that such differences are precisely why it is so important for them to try to participate in a simulation, but remember that you, as a leader, may yourself be perceived as a figure of authority who must be obeyed. At any rate, do not force a participant to play; the experience might actually be damaging rather than helpful.

Do not force a participant to play; the experience might actually be damaging rather than helpful.

Typical Behaviors to Watch For as a Function of Real Culture

This is a good place to recall that the synthetic culture profiles only relate to one aspect of social life. The interactions during the simulation require the participants to enact whole persons. This means they have to work out their behavior regarding the other four aspects (dimensions) of social life that are not in their culture profile. As a rule, the way that they do this is to behave in their accustomed ways as long as they don't contradict their profile.

The extent to which participants unknowingly enact their normal mode of social interaction while in their synthetic culture roles is striking. This is not to say that every participant from a certain country behaves in the same way; nothing could be further from the truth! Yet the overall tendency is clear.

Coloring Synthetic Culture with Real Culture. Participants who role-play a synthetic culture that they feel to be "strange" sometimes overdo it. For instance, Anglo people who play a Collec synthetic culture have a tendency to act in a feminine way. People from cultures of small power distance have a tendency to enact Hipow culture in a caricatured masculine way, the leader being bossy and the others feeling frustrated. Bossy individuals tend to grab the leader role in Hipow teams. Hipow team

The extent to which participants unknowingly enact their normal mode of social interaction while in their synthetic culture roles is striking.

members not in a leadership position sometimes start bossing high-status individuals from visiting teams around; this, of course, directly violates their profile. Hipow individuals are supposed to be very respectful of high-status visitors.

Wanting to Win. Participants from countries that are high on the masculinity and individualism scales will, without thinking, set their sights on winning the game if there is a quantitative criterion such as net gain or turnover. They will break the rules without ado and charge full speed ahead in achieving their objectives. It may be quite a job to get them to relinquish their roles after the simulation is over and debriefing has begun.

Facilitating the Simulation

Walking Around. The directions for this simulation should be clear to the participants so that you are free to walk around unobtrusively, get an overall impression of how the simulation is proceeding, and attend to any problems that might arise. "Sniffing" the atmosphere of each interaction in the simulation can be very valuable for facilitating the debriefing. If you announce beforehand that you will be circulating "invisibly" and if you adopt a silent and encouraging attitude, participants will not be disturbed and will hardly notice you. If anything, they will feel safer if they see that the simulation leader has not forgotten them.

Do not have side conversations with other simulation leaders within sight or hearing of the participants. This will certainly distract them.

The Role of Observers. As mentioned earlier, it is useful to have an observer with every team. Observers can focus on items that you wish to highlight during debriefing. Their assignment can range from very broad to very specific. Depending of the aims of the simulation, they can, for instance, focus on general characteristics such as the dynamics of a meeting, the symbolic use of space, nonverbal behaviors, misinterpretations, and so forth. They might try to establish the correspondence between the process of the meeting (the sequence of events and interactions) and the outcome of the meeting (i.e., agreement, puzzlement, or hostility). Or they might try to ascertain the role of an individual character, personal or interpersonal history, real culture, and synthetic culture in determining the process and outcome of the meeting. They might also focus on specific aspects such as turn taking, interrupting, the division of speaking time among participants, the use of specific words, and so forth.

Observers can also decide which team receives the synthetic culture prize. If so, they should carefully justify their decision during the debriefing.

Disturbances. Minimize the number of possible disturbances. Make sure, for example, that participants have their mobile phones turned off. If a participant cannot guarantee full participation, give him or her a role that can be omitted without harm.

If disturbances such as mobile phone calls cannot be avoided, ask each team to comment on how it perceives such interruptions from the point of view of its synthetic culture. Because this task forces the team to tackle an immediately relevant and real problem, it can be a very valuable exercise. There is, however, a risk of embarrassing participants during the simulation if they receive urgent or troubling calls while others around them are playacting a response to that call.

Questions and Dropping Out. Make sure that you or another facilitator can confidently answer difficult questions about the content matter of the simulation and that one—possibly the same individual—can do this for the synthetic cultures. This becomes very pressing when a participant revolts against the simulation through challenging questions or by dropping out. The best way to handle this is usually not to interrupt the simulation, but to take the participant aside and listen. Often the cause of the upset is that the simulated culture is too sharply at odds with the participant's reality—or too close to it. With luck the participant will continue playing after a private conversation. If not, you could ask the participant whether he or she wishes to be allotted some time during debriefing. The event will probably provide some very good material for debriefing. This debriefing can relate to the participant's revolt and to the fact that the objection was raised in the first place. Challenging the simulation is in itself a symbolic gesture that is perceived very differently in different cultures. Participants from individualist, small-power distance, masculine cultures are most likely to object to some aspect of the simulation because objecting to what leaders propose agrees with their cultural values.

Changing the Rules Midstream. Teams may take liberties and initiatives that you won't anticipate. As long as these are in the spirit of their synthetic cultures and do not disrupt the simulation, such spontaneous changes are strongly encouraged. They can add meaning to the simulation, particularly to the debriefing.

Debriefing the Simulation

Debriefing is a term used to describe everything that happens after the role playing finishes and before the players leave. It consists of a number of activities, usually conducted in a group session, and should take at least 30 percent of the total time. Debriefing starts when the participants are still emotionally invested in their roles and in the events that took place during the simulation. At the end of the debriefing, participants have all distanced themselves from their roles and hopefully have drawn some lessons from the exercise.

Your most important first act should be to emphasize that from this moment on, participants are no longer in their roles, that the simulation is over. If you don't make this clear up front, some of the participants may stay in role and can carry remaining resentments or misunderstandings away with them rather than learning from those reactions.

The structure of the debriefing depends on the particular simulation and on the achievement (or not) of the aims for which you played it. Some likely aspects follow.

Debriefing starts when the participants are still emotionally invested in their roles and in the events that took place during the simulation.

Miniature Debriefings during the Simulation

If the simulation consists of several rounds or meetings, a short debriefing session of this kind can be held within each team after each meeting. If an observer is present, he or she can conduct this miniature within-team evaluation. At the end of each cross-cultural meeting in which representatives have visited foreign teams, allow the visitors to return to their home cultures and give an account of the interaction with the foreign team while still playing their role and before letting the observer take over the debriefing. In this way participants have an opportunity to put into words their experience of culture conflict and frustration from the perspective of their synthetic culture.

Letting Off Steam

The more heated a simulation becomes, the harder it is for players to collect their wits for the debriefing. Before the participants can achieve the distance needed for reflection, they must have an opportunity to vent their emotions about what happened during the simulation—ergo, discuss feelings first. This need not be a very formal aspect of the debriefing. It can start with a short break during which players will no doubt spontaneously start discussing or arguing with one another about what happened from their point of view.

Discuss feelings first.

Winning and Losing

When all have had their say, it is time to start analyzing in a structured way what happened in the simulated world. If there is a win/lose element to the simulation, bring that up first. In all likelihood this will lead to more emotional expression, and those who have not won are likely to take it out on those who did. For participants from masculine cultures in particular, you may want to remind them that losing the game is not at all bad, because they may learn a great deal from losing.

Processes and Outcomes

It can be valuable to focus the analysis by using a presentation device that allows you to summarize the process and outcome of the activity. Now is the time for the observers to present any data they were instructed to collect during the simulation. The observers' objective observations can be compared with the players' feelings about the simulation events.

Be sure to focus on how events were *perceived* by all those who were present, not on what happened. Two different synthetic culture teams are likely to have perceived the same events in very different ways. It is particularly interesting to get the perceptions of both parties in cross-cultural meetings. In all likelihood a feeling of mutual estrangement will be manifest. In one debriefing, one observer exclaimed to another, "You must have been at a different meeting!"

Focus on how events were perceived by all those who were present, not on what happened.

Debriefing Questions

General questions:
- How did it *feel* to be a member of your synthetic culture? Was this the same for all members? Why (not)?
- Would your team's synthetic culture bring desirable traits to international organizations? Why?
- Did your real culture influence the way in which you enacted your synthetic culture role? How?
- What determined the course of the simulation: the players' personalities, the instructions, the synthetic cultures, or the true cultures?

Questions about single-culture teams:
- How did your team's synthetic culture influence the process of cooperation within your team?
- If teams had to invent, design, or plan something, did their synthetic culture have an influence on the result?

Questions about mixed-culture meetings:
- How did you feel in the presence of the people from other

EXPLORING CULTURE

synthetic cultures? Did you experience estrangement, frustration, or amusement?

- How did your team's synthetic culture influence the process of cooperating with "foreign" teams?
- Did misunderstandings occur? If so, why? Did misunderstandings arise over what was said or done (e.g., "Let me take you outside") or over what was intended (e.g., a private conversation or a fight)?
- Did you experience *cognitive* conflict, that is, disagreements about content matter? Did you experience *affective* conflict, in other words, a tense atmosphere or hostilities? How were the two related? How was it handled?

Questions comparing meetings:
- What were the dynamics of each "cross-cultural" meeting? What caused these dynamics? Can you pinpoint key events?
- Which synthetic cultures went well together, which did not, and why?

At the end of this phase of the debriefing, all participants should have achieved sufficient distance to be able to identify the causes of disagreement and frustration during the simulation and to see how the differing synthetic culture values contributed to their differing perceptions of the same events.

Linking the Simulation with Everyday Life

Now is the time to link the simulation experiences to the participants' everyday lives. The extent to which this can be done depends largely on the type of audience, notably the mix of nationalities present. Here are some possible issues to address:
- The synthetic cultures are deliberately artificial. When you play a synthetic culture, you are obsessed with just one aspect of social life. In real life, culture is multidimensional, a mix of characteristics of the five dimensions and their associated properties. For instance, a masculine culture that is also collectivistic will feel very different from one that is

individualistic. How do the dimensions interact in real cultures? Can you see how players from different real cultures have enacted the same synthetic culture profile in different ways during the simulation?

- If you have had cross-cultural experience, does the simulation help you to consider it in a new light? Can you interpret incidents from your experience in a more satisfactory way if you assume that the people you were dealing with were "acting out a different synthetic culture"?

- What conclusions can you draw for your future behavior in your working or social life? Can you formulate a list of dos and don'ts?

To make a concluding statement you could use the triad, awareness—knowledge—skills. The participants are by now *aware* that national culture determines the rules of the social game. They *know* the five major issues that constitute the dimensions of culture. They have acquired *skills* with the synthetic cultures through practice and are now better prepared to communicate across cultures in the real world. Ideally, they will never forget to find out by what social rules other people behave before trying to make sense of what they do.

If the simulation is new, you could now ask them whether it could be improved if you played it again.

Now we are ready to turn our attention to actual simulations. The two that follow are fully documented and ready to play as they exist. You can also use them, however, as a source of inspiration to create your own cross-cultural simulation game. We ordered the two simulations roughly by duration and level of difficulty. The first one is short and easy; the second one, longer and more complex.

Chapter 9

The Trade Mission

This is a straightforward synthetic culture simulation about trade negotiations; in fact, simulations hardly come any less complicated.

Basic Data

Objective: to practice cross-cultural negotiation

Target audience: anybody

Preparation time for participants: 15 minutes

Briefing and setup time: 5 minutes

Playing time: 30 minutes

Debriefing time: 30 minutes to 2 hours

Number of players: 8 to 100, in an even number of teams of 3 to 5 persons plus one observer per team

Materials required for players: synthetic culture profiles (see chapter 3); see also page 216 for Rules of Play Handout

Materials required for simulation director: briefing and debriefing instructions

Equipment/room setup required: room for plenary briefing and debriefing plus small rooms for face-to-face negotiation

Description

A number of delegations (three to five persons each) attend a large international trade event at which they hope to do business with the delegation of a foreign country they know little about. The delegations have a brief meeting during which they decide on what product they want to sell, read and practice their synthetic cultures, and devise sales strategies. Then they have a second meeting in which they negotiate with the foreign delegation. Because both delegations want to sell rather than to buy, there is a threat of conflict. The following three sections are to be used as handouts for participants.

Roles

There is an even number of delegations consisting of three to five members in the following roles:
- The head of the delegation, a highly placed and renowned diplomat
- A captain of industry
- One to two lesser but eager executives

In addition an observer is appointed to every delegation. The observer does not participate in the simulation. He or she sits and watches until the debriefing at the end of the simulation, at which time the observers get the floor to summarize from an objective point of view what they have observed. The observer should be particularly attentive to the relative importance of the players' personalities, roles, and synthetic culture profiles in determining the course of both meetings. Also, the observer will be watching for differences between the within-culture and the between-cultures settings.

Synthetic Cultures

Each team will be formed on the basis of one of the ten possible synthetic culture profiles, depending on the audience. Use the profiles from chapter 3, and you might also distribute the opening section of that chapter if you allocate more reading time.

You can adapt the choice of synthetic cultures to your didactic aims. Chapter 8 gives some pointers for determining your choice.

Timetable

Here is a minimal timetable for this simulation. Follow it if the simulation is used as an "appetizer." If there is more time, increase the time available to the participants to acquaint themselves with the synthetic cultures, for example, by having them do acculturation exercises before having the within-team meeting or asking them to plan more detailed sales strategies. Also increase the time for debriefing. One can easily spend a whole day on this simulation.

5 minutes: Introduce the synthetic cultures and the simulation.

10 minutes: Form teams on the basis of the synthetic cultures of the participants' or your choice. The teams will be called Country 1, 2, and so on. The teams decide on the division of roles: head of delegation, captain of industry, lesser executive(s), and observer. Ask participants to read the profile of their culture.

15 minutes: During the single-team meeting, members determine what product to offer. The only condition is that the product must be compatible with the team's national culture. Teams then make up sales strategies based on their synthetic cultures and practice interacting.

20 minutes: Designate half of the teams (the receiving teams) to remain where they are in their breakout rooms. Instruct the other half to go to the large group room and wait. A member of each of the receiving teams goes to the large group room to invite one of the teams that is waiting there. The two-team meetings then begin, whereby each set of two teams establishes a trading relationship and negotiates some actual business. The teams do not know, nor should they talk about, each other's synthetic culture.

10 minutes: End of the simulation. Gather the entire group for a plenary session during which each of the observers briefly sums up what he or she has seen. They speak in twos according to which two-team meeting they attended.

30 minutes to 2 hours: Debriefing. Although we give the minimum debriefing time as 30 minutes, we suggest that you use more time to take full advantage of the learning possible.

2 minutes: Make a couple of summary comments and end the session.

Debriefing

Here is a possible format for making notes on the blackboard at the start of the debriefing. The observers will provide the data for this matrix. The data listed are fictitious.

Team	Synthetic Culture	Product	Outcome	Satisfaction	Process	Stereotype
1	Hipow	pyramids	No deal yet; to be continued	Moderate	Restrained	Uptight
2	Femi	nurses		High		Uncivilized but nice
3	Mascu	guns	No deal; Mascus ran off	Very low	Noisy, then hostile	Pushy
4	Lopow	mobiles		Felt insulted		Chaotic

Here is what the column headers denote:
- Team: the team's name or number. Each team has one row, and teams that were in a meeting together have rows next to one another.
- Synthetic culture: the team's synthetic culture.
- Product: the product that the team decided to sell during the first meeting.

- Outcome: the outcome of the meeting. This is *not per team but per two-team meeting!*
- Level of satisfaction: an evaluation in role regarding whether the team was happy with the outcome of the meeting. This evaluation is *per team.*
- Process: an evaluation *by the observers* about the atmosphere during the meeting. This is also *per meeting, not per team*.
- Perception by others: an evaluative statement about each team *as the other synthetic culture perceived them* during the meeting.

In chapter 8 you will find a number of questions that will help make sense of the simulation and link it to everyday life. You can use all or some of these questions to structure the debriefing.

The Trade Mission: Rules of Play
Handout

You are a member of a trade delegation from your country. You are attending an important international trade event at which you intend to conduct some good business. One other country in particular has caught your attention. Although your country has had little to do with this country, that could change. You hope to establish a positive trading relationship.

Your team will hold an initial ten-minute meeting in order to practice your synthetic culture and determine what product to offer. It could be anything. Some possible examples: flowers, refrigerators, wrist-worn communicators, zeppelins, or health-care programs. The product will of course be compatible with your national (synthetic) culture. You will be proud to be able to offer your product for sale. After you have chosen your country's product, plan sales strategies compatible with your synthetic culture.

Then you will visit or receive a foreign delegation for a joint team meeting to establish a trading relationship and to negotiate some actual business. You believe they might be willing to buy a sizable quantity of goods or services from your country right now, and you would like to conclude a deal during this meeting. A success would be good for your country as well as for your team's company and careers.

There are two preconditions, however. First, you are not interested in buying more than a symbolic amount of their product, which your country is not in need of, in return. Second, the instinctive feeling between you and the other country's delegation needs to be right if the relationship is to become an enduring one.

Chapter 10

Follow-the-Sun Global Technology Team*

Follow-the-Sun is a simulation based on different time zones. A global virtual team working at three sites, each one in a different time zone and of a different culture, will simulate follow-the-sun project work using only e-mail—with its endemic communication and cultural difficulties. An intervention is introduced before the last round to improve teamwork. The task is to draw a map of the world, a task that includes three stages: vision, design, and drawing.

Basic Data

Objective: to experience the specific problems of working under time stress in different time, place, and culture design teams

Target audience: people who are doing or will have to do follow-the-sun project work

Preparation time for participants: none

Briefing and setup time: a few minutes; 15 minutes for the project manager

---

* By Erran Carmel, Gert Jan Hofstede, and Shawn Bates. John Allee, Roger Volkema (both of American University), and participants in the SIETAR-USA conference, November 2000, also contributed to the content in this exercise.

Playing time: 105 minutes

Debriefing time: 45 minutes

Number of players: 10 to 20, equally divided into three site teams. If you have several more than 20 participants, assign the extras to be observers of the three site teams.

Materials required for players: lots of easel paper, colored markers, and tape; also the profile of the synthetic culture that each person is assigned to.

Materials required for simulation director: a loud alarm of some kind to indicate the end of each round. We suggest that you bring along an accurate map of the world for reference in the debriefing. Note that different world projections are common in different parts of the globe.

Equipment/room setup required: a location in which there are three separate areas (we'll called them stations, since the teams rotate) for each of the site teams to meet without distraction from the other two teams; one of these stations is the "Build Station," where the "awake" team works.

Background

With rapid globalization and high-tech development, many projects are now dispersed across countries. In fact, among multinationals and leading technology companies, projects often collaborate across three or four or five different national sites (Carmel 1999).

While dispersed project work is problematic, as described below, globally dispersed technology work has some potential advantages—the most attractive of which is follow-the-sun design and development, also known as round-the-clock work. The concept of a follow-the-sun schedule is illustrated by a concrete example. When the California site finishes its work for the day, it sends its work, such as design modules or source code, to its sister team in Bangalore, India (ten and one-half time zones away). As members of this site finish their morning tea or coffee, they read through the materials written by their American colleagues and begin their work where the California team has stopped. As the sun sets in Bangalore, the local site finishes its day's tasks, reversing the information flow, albeit with its day's worth of added work, to California. And so it goes. The (theoretical) result is a 50 percent reduction in the product's time to market. If 3 site teams are involved instead of just 2, and if they are situated appropriately across time zones, then the project team can work three shifts in 24 hours; time to market is reduced 67 percent.

However, a globally dispersed development team presents problems that do not exist for traditional teams. Much of the communication between the site teams is conducted via e-mail, which, obviously, lacks many of the possibilities of face-to-face communication. When we communicate face-to-face, we transmit much more than the objective text of our message. As much as 80 percent of the message is nonverbal, that is, body language, facial expression, the tone or inflection of our voice, and the context. Nonverbal communication is particularly important to "high context" or collectivist cultures, mainly those outside the North American/Northern European axis. In contrast, e-mail messages are often vague or obtuse, they lack the information richness of face-to-face communication, it is harder to add emphasis, and we don't have the luxury of receiving instant clarification. This is particularly annoying in a situation where participants are forced to communicate across language boundaries and cannot use their mother tongue. Also, the visual process of step-by-step development of a product is lost because the next site team sees only the end-of-the-day results, not the interim work.

Funneling all of the communication between the site teams into written electronic mail messages is the centerpiece of this simulation exercise. The language could be any language that is common across the teams, but is most likely to be English.

> *A participant in a cross-cultural follow-the-sun simulation commented: "We felt excluded, like our views did not matter because they didn't seem to be being responded to.... Our communication was stifled by the 'e-mail' format – we really needed to be able to talk with the project manager or the other groups."*

High-technology teams, particularly those working on design projects (e.g., research and development), require a great deal of communication. One of the main purposes of communication is coordination. Coordination is the act of integrating each task and organizational unit so that it contributes to the overall objective. High-technology product development work is a highly complex activity and requires many small acts of coordination and problem solving. Many small adjustments are made and frequent problem solving is required of the people working on various aspects of the project. When everyone is located along the same corridor, team members make these adjustments themselves, quickly and informally. When members are far away from each other, these numerous small adjustments and fixes are often not made until late into the project and hence add to the cost or to-market time.

Finally, globally dispersed technology teams, by necessity, need to deal with cross-cultural communication issues, adding another layer of complexity to an already complicated situation.

During the life cycle of any product or system, it goes through a set of generic stages. The first stage is a high-level, abstract stage, which in this exercise we label "vision." The second stage is a "design" stage (which in the real world involves multiple substages). The third stage is the drawing stage. For a tangible product, this might be building a prototype. The *Follow-the-Sun* simulation emulates these three generic stages.

Description

In this simulation, we refer to the different sites as "site teams" because, at least in theory, all of them belong to one dispersed team. The task of the multisite team is to draw a map of the world. The objectives are (1) accuracy in geography and place-names and (2) an artistic theme. These objectives must be made clear to the participants.

Communication between sites will take place via simulated e-mail. During its "workday," each team leaves notes (on easel paper taped to the walls) to simulate electronic mail messages to the next follow-the-sun team members. No direct communication between teams is allowed between sites during the simulation unless specified by the facilitator. A surprise intervention (bringing the participants together) is part of the simulation, but do not communicate this to the participants ahead of time.

There are 3 site teams. Each unit is composed of one leader and one or more geographers and artists. There is also 1 project manager (PM) from the headquarters (HQ) country who rotates with the headquarters unit. The PM has responsibility for the entire project.

Each site team will choose or be assigned a synthetic culture. The three cultures are HQ, Collec, and Uncavo. Brief scripts are presented on pages 227–28. (The latter two are also described on pages 96–97 and 105–106.) The teams do not disclose their cultural values to the other teams (in other words, they should not exchange their cultural descriptions). The HQ site team is assigned a Western-style culture, as is the PM, which is typical for most high-tech virtual teams.

Additional Information for the Simulation Leader

The Build Site is the room where participants construct the artifact, in this case the world map. This should be the site where the HQ culture meets for the first time. It is important that participants know which site they will build in before the simulation begins, to avoid any confusion and to ease the team planning process.

During the simulation, the facilitator is very active, keeping track of time, enforcing and interpreting the rules, and most important, shuffling the site teams between stations at the end of each of the five-minute periods. We strongly recommend that you have an assistant simulation leader to help with keeping time, switching the teams, and generally making the exercise run more smoothly. This will free the lead facilitator to make more observations about team dynamics and the overall process of the simulation.

Some ambiguity is part of the point of this exercise. It leads to different individual interpretations of the simulation that will become valuable material for debriefing.

Role: Project Manager

There is only one specialized role in this simulation: the project manager. You should select a PM from among the participants in the exercise ahead of time. You can do this by appointment or by asking for volunteers. The PM writes the vision statement and decides on the division of the tasks.

Allow about 15 minutes for the PM to write the vision statement. You can let the HQ team work on it collectively or, alternatively, let the PM work alone, as you wish. We suggest that the vision statement be hand-copied, distributed to the 3 site teams, and pasted on the wall. Being the PM is a stressful job, and this should be noted to the participant who has volunteered or been selected for the position. Think carefully before deciding to let participants volunteer for this role. An ineffective PM can be detrimental to the experience of the group. There should be an opportunity at this point for the PM to back out and a new PM be selected. Here is a quote from one PM:

> "I felt a lot of time pressure with having to write everything out three times. And I wanted to visit all the groups, but that wasn't allowed. And then I wanted to telephone, but that didn't seem to be possible either.... I felt very much out of touch with the other teams, though we in the Lopow site team were doing well."

Once the PM has completed writing the vision statement, he or she joins the HQ team in the Build Site (if he has written the statement alone).

Role: Team Leader

Each team has a leader. The PM is, as mentioned earlier, the leader of the HQ team. The other two teams select a leader. This leader has no preassigned role.

Role: Observer

If you assign observers to the teams, you can instruct them to look for the following:

Work partitioning/task allocation:
- How was allocation of tasks handled, and why was it done this way?
- How was the task partitioned? Were there modules or phases?
- Did it work? Why or why not?

Architecture/vision:
- Who set the vision? PM or collectively?
- What was the effect of the team's synthetic culture on the way of working? On the outcome?

Culture:
- How did your culture perceive other site cultures?
- Did different sites work differently? How?

Communication between sites:
- Face-to-face versus written "e-mails": What worked, and what did not?

Leadership:
- What was the role of PM and team leaders? Were they dominant in each of the sites?

Steps of Play

Tentative Schedule

Stage	Minutes	Composition
Before the simulation: assign the PM and let PM write mission statement.	15	PM
Introduce the simulation and explain the rules and the synthetic cultures.	15	Everyone together
Assign teams.	5	Everyone together
Practice the cultures in each site team. Ask the teams to create a plan for the project based on the design preferences of their synthetic culture. They will discuss the vision in their culture roles.	10	By site team
Round One: Design Stage begins. No work on the actual artifact (the map) is allowed yet. Site teams make one full rotation. (1) The team at each site read the e-mail (the vision) from PM, discusses it, and responds by "e-mail." (2) Each team rotates one station, reads both e-mails, discusses, and responds by e-mail. (3) Each team rotates one station (now each team will have visited all three sites), reads the 3 e-mails, and responds by e-mail.	15	By site team
Round Two: Build Stage begins. Participants work in rotation on the actual artifact, 5 minutes per site. Site teams not working in the Build Site (the one designated site room) are "sleeping" and should not engage in work activities. (They could do group exercises, e.g., those in chapter 7.) The HQ team starts building at the Build Site, then Uncavo, then Collec. The site teams start to work. Each simulated working day lasts 5 minutes, after which the team leaves the work with some e-mail for the following team.†	15	By site team

---

† The site team from headquarters is treated in the same way as the other teams.

Intervention: The simulation leader asks the PM to call the site teams together for an unannounced face-to-face meeting. Use some expressions such as "We have received additional budget to fly everybody to Acapulco for a meeting." This is the point in the project where the teams actually meet face-to-face for the first time to work out their differences and to develop a shared model for their work. How the meeting is conducted should be up to the PM. The site teams will, of course, stay in their synthetic culture roles during the meeting. Depending on how much time you have, you might allow extra time here.	15	Everyone together
Round Three: The site teams put to advantage the benefits they gained from the intervention. The HQ team goes first, then Uncavo, then Collec.	15	By site team
Debriefing	45	Everyone together

Debriefing

Participants will be tired after the exercise; it is draining, trying to deal with so many variables while working under such time pressure. This is an expected and desired outcome. Working with other cultures and trying to break though a communication breakdown require a great deal of energy, particularly in the learning stages, which is where *Follow-the-Sun* takes place.

The PM is a critical component of *Follow-the-Sun*. This person needs to be treated with care by the simulation leaders, particularly during the debriefing. He or she may well become more emotionally vested in the exercise—and in the opinion of the group regarding his or her performance—than any other participant.

This list of questions should guide your debriefing.

1. Ask the project manager about his or her perception of the project and the workings of the teams. This will help this individual to "derole" and to vent any frustrations about personal performance.

2. Ask each team to evaluate the final product from the perspective of its synthetic culture. Is it a good map? Is it an aesthetically pleasing map?

3. Ask the group about its perceptions of project management, coordination, and communication issues. If you had observers, let them comment on these issues first, then let the teams respond.

4. Ask the participants whether they made assumptions about what they thought of the other teams, their cultures, and their work ethic.

5. Did e-mail stifle communication? (Yes! In fact this is a part of the simulation. Deciphering the meaning of the e-mail messages sent among the teams is an integral part of the team experience and a valuable lesson for everyone in the exercise.)

6. How was the vision communicated? Could it have been communicated differently? Would the PM have done it differently knowing, now, some more about the other cultures? Discuss just how much impact that initial vision and its interpretation can have on the group's understanding of the whole project.

7. What was the effect of the face-to-face meeting? (Presumably, the third round was considerably more productive than the second because it took place after the face-to-face meeting.)

8. What are the most significant insights about global technology teams and e-mail that have come from this exercise?

Synthetic Cultures

The three site teams are assigned to three synthetic cultures: HQ, Collec, and Uncavo. The characteristics of each culture include general cultural attributes and those that involve design aesthetics. The design aesthetics are introduced to create cultural behaviors specific to design. Specific-culture briefing tables are found on pages 227–228. As you can see by comparing the profiles with those of chapter 3, HQ culture assembles elements of Lopow, Indiv, and Unctol, reflecting a Western culture pattern. Each participant who is assigned to one of these synthetic cultures receives a photocopy of the description of his or her culture.

It is possible, depending on the audience, to work with synthetic culture profiles other than the three given here. However, no perspectives on design for the other seven synthetic cultures are included here. You would need to add these if you feel confident doing so.

HQ Culture

Dimension	Preferences	Dislikes
General Culture	Decentralization Consult with subordinates Fairness Task focus Precision in communication Innovation Experimentation	Difficulty with hierarchy, orders, commands, beating around the bush, formalities, becoming emotional
Design and Aesthetics	Lots of white space	

Uncavo Culture

Dimension	Preferences	Dislikes
General Culture	Rules, even those that never work Emotional verbal style Our truth is the only one Predictability Strong national pride	The unfamiliar Ambiguity Creativity Flexibility
Design and Aesthetics	Sharp edges Straight lines Strong contrast of colors	

Collec Culture

Dimension	Preferences	Dislikes
General Culture	Harmony Face (don't insult others) Tradition Relationships Imprecise speaking with lots of nonverbal cues Respect for elders	Self-interest Low-context behavior Negotiations Confrontation, talking to someone with whom you disagree
Design and Aesthetics	Circles The color red	

Variations

An alternative task that we have experimented with is asking the group to build a "model city," requiring the participants to use wooden blocks, strips to simulate roads, toy cars, and so forth. This task requires more preparation because many kinds of materials and tools are needed. The Build Site could be the art room in a school. More time would be needed for the simulated working days. This is a very richly symbolic task. There are many degrees of freedom in designing a city, because a city can hold buildings or infrastructure for just about all the social activities that people can engage in.

References

A wealth of excellent books and training materials exist, much more than can be mentioned here. In this list we limit ourselves to material that is closely related to the book, historically, or that we recommend for further reading. For current information about cross-cultural simulation gaming, contact ISAGA, NASAGA, or SIETAR.

Barna, LaRay. 1982. "Stumbling Blocks in Intercultural Communication." In *Intercultural Communication: A Reader*, 330–38, edited by Larry Samovar and Richard Porter. Belmont, CA: Wadsworth.

Bhawuk, Dharm P. S. 1998. "The Role of Culture Theory in Cross-Cultural Training: A Multimethod Study of Culture-Specific, Culture General, and Culture-Theory-Based Assimilators." *Journal of Cross-Cultural Psychology 29*, 630–55.

Brislin, Richard W., and Dharm P. S. Bhawuk. 1999. "Cross-Cultural Training: Research and Innovations." In *Social Psychology and Cultural Context*, edited by J. Adamopoulos and Y. Kashimads, 205–16. Thousand Oaks, CA: Sage.

Carmel, Erran. 1999. *Global Software Teams: Collaborating Across Borders and Time Zones*. Upper Saddle River, NJ: Prentice-Hall.
A book for those who are involved in follow-the-sun design work. Practical without being simplistic.

Fowler, Sandra M., and Monica G. Mumford, eds. 1995; 1999. *Intercultural Sourcebook: Cross-Cultural Training Methods.* Vols. 1 and 2. Yarmouth, ME: Intercultural Press.

Greenblat, Cathy Stein, and Richard D. Duke. 1981. *Principles and Practices of Gaming–Simulation.* Beverly Hills, CA: Sage.

An authoritative guide to simulation gaming.

Grove, Cornelius, and Willa Hallowell. 2001. *Randömia Balloon Factory: A Unique Simulation for Working across the Cultural Divide.* Yarmouth, ME: Intercultural Press.

Hofstede, Geert. 2001. *Culture's Consequences: Software of the Mind.* 2d ed. Thousand Oaks, CA: Sage.

Twenty years after the first edition, Geert Hofstede reviews the field in this scholarly volume, including many hundreds of studies on national culture that were carried out since the first edition appeared.

———. 1991. *Cultures and Organizations: Software of the Mind.* London: McGraw-Hill.

The "popular" edition of Geert Hofstede's five-dimension model of national culture. Many reprints and translations are available.

Hofstede, Gert Jan, and Paul B. Pedersen. 1999. "Synthetic Cultures: Intercultural Learning through Simulation Games." *Simulation and Gaming* 30, no. 4, 415–40.

The article that prompted this book.

Ivey, Allen E., and M. B. Ivey. 1999. *Intentional Interviewing and Counseling.* Pacific Grove, CA: Brooks/Cole Publishing Company.

Ivey, Allen E., Paul B. Pedersen, and M. B. Ivey. In press. *Intentional Group Counseling: A Microskills Approach.* Pacific Grove, CA: Brooks/Cole Publishing Company.

Landis, Dan, and Ravi S. Bhagat. 1996. *Handbook of Intercultural Training.* 2d ed. Thousand Oaks, CA: Sage.

Nipporica Associates and Dianne Hofner Saphiere. 1997. *Ecotonos: A Multicultural Problem-Solving Simulation.* 2d ed. Yarmouth, ME: Intercultural Press.

Pedersen, Paul B. 2000. *Hidden Messages in Culture-Centered Counseling: A Triad Training Model.* Beverly Hills, CA: Sage.

Pedersen, Paul B., and Allen E. Ivey. 1993. *Culture-Centered Counseling and Interviewing Skills: A Practical Guide.* Westport CT: Greenwood Press.
The book that introduced synthetic cultures in counseling.

Shirts, R. Garry. 1977. *BaFá BaFá: A Cross Culture Simulation.* San Diego, CA: Simulation Training Systems.
This game could be called the mother of all culture simulation games.

Storti, Craig. 1999. *Figuring Foreigners Out: A Practical Guide.* Yarmouth, ME: Intercultural Press.
A do-it-yourself book full of living exercises. It deals at length with the various facets of the individualism/ collectivism dimension. It includes an extensive list of sources for further reading.

Thiagarajan, Sivasailam, and Barbara Steinwachs. 1990. *Barnga: A Simulation Game on Cultural Clashes.* Yarmouth, ME: Intercultural Press.

Web References

soeweb.syr.edu/chs/pedersen/index.html
   Paul Pedersen's Website
www.geerthofstede.com
   portal to the work of Geert Hofstede
www.info.wau.nl/people/gertjan/gj-uk.htm
   Gert Jan's Website with exercises and simulations
www.interculturalpress.com
   Intercultural Press Website
www.stsintl.com/business/bafa.html
   Simulation Training Systems (BaFa BaFa)

About the Authors

Gert Jan Hofstede, principal author of *Exploring Culture*, is a cross-cultural trainer and teacher in addition to being a senior researcher in information technology at Wageningen University in the Netherlands and a visiting lecturer at the London School of Economics and elsewhere. In his own words he is "an inspired teacher, sometimes even an actor." He has cut across disciplines throughout his adult life, applying insights from biology, anthropology, social psychology, and business sciences to communication contexts. Gert Jan has a Ph.D. in production planning from Wageningen University. He has full mastery of English, Dutch, and French and is fluent in Danish and German. A member of the International Simulation and Gaming Association, he has created numerous games and simulations that apply his father's (Geert Hofstede) work on the dimensions of culture in realistic social and business situations. He delivers these gaming events at international conferences, for universities, and for multinational companies.

Paul B. Pedersen has had a long and notable career in the areas of counselor education, cross-cultural psychology, communication, intercultural training, international education, and constructive conflict management, among others. He has been an instructor, foreign student adviser, professor, trainer, researcher, consultant, and senior Fulbright scholar. His work has taken him all over the world. Paul holds a Ph.D. in Asian Studies and a master's degree in counseling and student personnel psychology. A prolific writer, Pedersen has authored or edited numerous books, chapters in books, and more than one hundred articles and monographs. In addition to *Counseling across Cultures*, he is also known for his *Handbook of Cross-Cultural Counseling and Therapy* and *Culture-Centered Counseling and Interviewing Skills*, coauthored with Allen Ivey.

Geert Hofstede is recognized internationally for having developed the first empirical model of "dimensions" of national culture, thus establishing a new paradigm for taking account of cultural elements in international economics, communication, and cooperation. Later on, he also developed a model of organizational cultures. He is professor emeritus of organizational anthropology and international management at Maastricht University in the Netherlands. He is presently affiliated with Tilburg University as senior fellow of the Institute for Research on Intercultural Cooperation and is an extra-mural fellow of the Center for Economic Research. He also served as an honorary professor at the University of Hong Kong from 1993 to 2000. Dr. Hofstede is a fellow of the Academy of Management in the United States and holds honorary doctorates from universities at Nyenrode, the Netherlands; Sofia, Bulgaria; Athens, Greece; and Gothenburg, Sweden. He has lectured at universities, training institutes, and corporations around the world and has served as a consultant to national and international business and government organizations, including the World Bank, OECD, Asian Productivity Organization, and the Commission of the European Union. He holds a Ph.D. in social psychology from the University of Groningen in the Netherlands. Hofstede's books have appeared in eighteen languages, and his articles have been published in journals in Europe, Asia, and North America. He is among the top fifty most often cited authors in the *Social Science Citation Index*, one of only a few non–Americans on the list.